The Civilization of the American Indian Series

(Complete list on page 128)

Tanaina Tales from Alaska

Tanaina Tales

from Alaska

by Bill Vaudrin

Introduction by Joan B. Townsend

UNIVERSITY OF OKLAHOMA PRESS
NORMAN

E
99
T /85
V3

Standard Book Number: 8061-0858-4

Library of Congress Catalog Card Number: 69-16717

For that copyrighted material that appeared in article form in *Viltis: A Folklore Magazine* (see pages xii–xiii) and used here in essentially original form, copyright assigned 1969 to University of Oklahoma Press, courtesy V. F. Beliagus, Editor of *Viltis*. New edition copyright 1969 by the University of Oklahoma Press, Publishing Division of the University. Composed and printed at Norman, Oklahoma, U.S.A., by the University of Oklahoma Press. First edition.

to

Walter and Annie Johnson

the very best people in the world

Preface

THE PRE-RUSSIAN CULTURE of the Lake Iliamna–Cook Inlet Tanaina is dead. A few songs and dances survive, a handful of legitimate artifacts, and a dissipating language, as tangible evidences of its once-glory and pathos. And we have the Russian records. But most of what is known today about the early Tanaina has been perpetuated in the villages through the oral tradition, itself fading.

Three kinds of stories are told by the old-timers: (1) true historical accounts—usually epic narratives of wars with the Aleuts or Russians, and sometimes of individual heroes who distinguished themselves in those wars; (2) cultural myths— tales involving spirits or beings, other than men and animals, which inhabit the earth;* (3) "legend-stories"—anecdotal narratives centered on a particular animal, or animals, common to the Tanaina country. This volume is a collection of the third type of story—the *suk-tu*.

In the days before the Russian encounter, *suk-tus* were told primarily to entertain and instruct (*dulce et utile*), and they are as apt to do so for today's audience as yesterday's. But their central value for the twentieth century may well consist in what was peripheral to the seventeenth—the incidental picture of life in the Tanaina world out of which the legends grew. The stories reflect both the thinking of their originators and the nature of the physical community and environment in which they lived.

Anachronisms such as "chair," "window," "ax," and "cabin" appear in some of the stories, and serve as an index to either their later genesis or their susceptibility to foreign influence. At any rate, these references are a part of the legends as they are told today, and I have denied myself the liberty of weeding them out.

* See my "The Amigook, the Eiukna, and the Joncha," *The Alaska Review*, Vol. I, No. 1 (Winter, 1963), 20–35.

I have attempted at all times to impart the original *sense* of the stories, both in choice of language and dramatic or moral intention, as it has been communicated to me by the old-timers. That is, I have tried to say what I think *they* were trying to say— about life and how life was. The great difficulty, challenge, and responsibility of a re-creator in my position involves, of course, being remedially aware of the cultural difference that exists between the world for which these stories were intended and that to which I now present them.

One device I have employed is use of vernacular and idiomatic expressions common among the old-timers in their daily speech patterns, particularly expressions which reappear consistently in the recounting of the legend-stories: "September-month," "forth and back," "cache house," "picking wood," "married up with," inviting someone to "sit up and eat," etc. My rationalization is that these are intercultural expressions of Russian or Indian idioms that are on their way to becoming anglicized, which have not yet passed the stage of transition where they are valuable as reflections of the culture from which they spring.

The stories appearing here come almost exclusively from Pedro Bay and Nondalton villages, two Tanaina communities in the Lake Iliamna region of southwestern Alaska (see map following). The people originally migrated into this area from the Kenai Peninsula, and still refer to themselves as "Kenai" Indians. They belong to the Athapascan language group, along with such other North American tribes as the Apaches and Navahos.

No words on a printed page could hope to recapture the spirit and immediacy of a firsthand telling of these stories by the people themselves. Steambaths and fish boats have played their parts for me—and gas lamps and Swede stoves, log houses and long winter nights. Many of my favorite hours were spent in the preparation of this collection of stories.

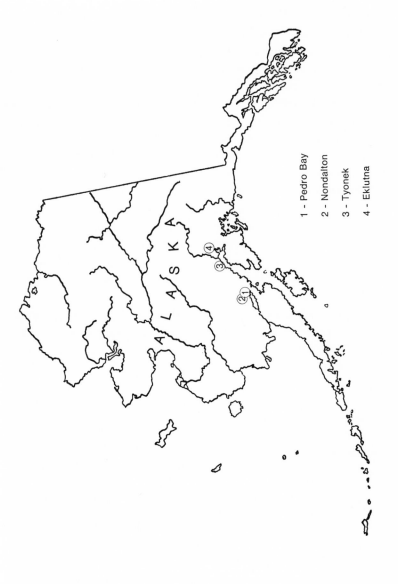

1 - Pedro Bay
2 - Nondalton
3 - Tyonek
4 - Eklutna

Deepest thanks to Michael A. and Jean Ricteroff, who have spent so many hours re-creating for me the days of the old time, and who are responsible for the plots of most of the stories as they appear here.

And to Walter and Annie Johnson, who first suggested the project of collecting the legends, and who have stood by me and been helpful in every way through its completion.

Also to the many friends at Pedro Bay, Nondalton, Eklutna, and Tyonek who have shared stories with me or given helpful advice and criticism, especially Rose Hedlund, Gillie Jacko, Gulia Delkettie, Logaria Foss, and the late Sophie Foss.

And to Joan Broom Townsend, anthropologist, for making available to me her unpublished doctoral dissertation concerning the ethnohistory, ecology, and cultural change of the Tanaina Indian in the Cook Inlet–Lake Iliamna region;

To Robert D. Bowen;

To Mr. V. F. (Vyts) Beliajus, editor of *Viltis* folklore magazine, for printing and releasing copyright privileges for: "The Wolverine Story" (Vol. XXIV, No. 4, December, 1965), "The First Beaver Story" (Vol. XXIV, No. 5, January–February, 1966), "The Fox Story" (Vol. XXIV, No. 6, March–April, 1966), "The Mouse Story" (Vol. XXV, No. 1, May, 1966), "The Second Beaver Story" (Vol. XXV, No. 2, June–September, 1966), "The Trout Story" (Vol. XXV, No. 3, October–November, 1966), "First Brown Bear Story" (Vol. XXV, No. 4, December, 1966), "The Loon Story" (Vol. XXV, No. 5, January–February, 1967), "The Black Bear Story" (Vol. XXV, No. 6, March–April, 1967), "The Lynx and the Wolverine," "The Second Eagle Story" (Vol. XXVI, No. 1, May, 1967), "The First Eagle Story," "The Loon Story" (Vol. XXVI, No. 2, June–September, 1967), "The Cat Story" (Vol. XXVI, No. 3, October–November, 1967), "The Porcupine and the Beaver" (Vol. XXVI, No. 4, December, 1967), and "The Sea Gull Story"

(Vol. XXVI, No. 5, January–February, 1968, and Vol. XXVI, No. 6, March–April, 1968).

To my mothers, Mrs. L. E. Bennett and Mrs. Philip S. Heid, for typing, proofreading, and textual criticism.

And to Betsy.

BILL VAUDRIN

Eagle River, Alaska
May 7, 1969

The Illustrations

The illustrations used throughout the book are not merely decorative devices, but are reproductions of cave paintings, thought to be at least several hundred years old, from Sadie Cove, Tuxedni Bay, and Clam Beach, all on Cook Inlet. They were drawn by the Kenai Indians (Tanaina Athapascans) who lived on the Inlet and, to my knowledge have never been reproduced before.

Some of the paintings are easily recognizable—a boat with men in it, a porpoise, a goose, a man, a bear—but others cannot be identified with certainty by either the descendants of the original artists or by anthropologists.

The artist who made the reproductions is Buck Hayden, who graduated from Alaska Methodist University in 1966 and received a Master of Fine Arts degree in painting from the University of Oregon in 1968. He has fished commercially on Cook Inlet for fifteen years.

BILL VAUDRIN

Contents

Map

Introduction

FOLK TALES ARE USUALLY ENTERTAINING in themselves, but they take on a deeper meaning when the reader has some knowledge of the way of life of the people who created them. It is my intention in these pages to provide a background for the tales that follow.

The Tanaina Indians have been given some fifty names by various authors since Europeans first discovered them, the most common of these being Kenaitze, Knaiakhotana, Tinnats, and Tanaina. To the people of southwestern Alaska, they are also known as the Kenai. In an anthropological study of their culture in the 1930's, Cornelius Osgood used the name "Tanaina" to refer to both the people and their language. Thus it was established in the anthropological literature.

The Tanaina are Athapascan members of the large Na-déné language family which also includes the Tlingit and Haida peoples in southeastern Alaska. Other Athapascans are found in western Canada and interior Alaska and in such far-flung places as northern California (Tolowa and other tribes) and the southwestern part of the United States (Navahos and Apaches). Although the Tanaina are more closely related linguistically to some of the Athapascans in central Canada, their culture is more like that of the Tlingit, whose environment is similar and with whom they probably share a common heritage.

The Tanaina occupy southwestern Alaska in the region surrounding Cook Inlet—in the Susitna River Valley, on Kenai Peninsula, and in the Iliamna Lake area. One Tanaina village is on Stony River, tributary to the Kuskokwim. During the nineteenth century, most of the Tanaina of the Iliamna region lived in the villages of Old Iliamna (on Iliamna Lake) and at Kijik (on Lake Clark). In the early twentieth century, they slowly abandoned these villages in favor of the modern Pedro Bay, on

Iliamna Lake, and Nondalton, on Sixmile Lake between Iliamna and Lake Clark. Approximately fifty Tanaina now live in Pedro Bay, and the larger Nondalton usually has a population of around two hundred.

Iliamna Lake is some ninety miles long and forty miles wide. The Tanaina inhabit the mountainous northeastern portion, which is covered with moderately heavy forests of spruce, cottonwood, birch, ash, willow, and other vegetation. This part of the lake lies only twelve miles over a portage from Cook Inlet. The Iliamna Tanaina, as well as the Kenai Peninsula Tanaina, are unique among Athapascans because, having moved to the coast, they are able to exploit maritime as well as lake, riverine, and interior environments.

Living near the Tanaina in the southern and western portions of Iliamna Lake and on Kodiak and adjacent islands are the Eskimos. In the past, the Tanaina fought with, acquired slaves from, occasionally intermarried with, and traded with these powerful Eskimos. In Tanaina culture, then, occurrences of Eskimo cultural traits are not surprising.

History

The Tanaina were already settled in the Cook Inlet-Iliamna region when they came into contact with Western civilization. Bering discovered Alaska in 1741, but it was not until 1784 that the Russian fur traders made their way up the Aleutian chain and built a permanent station at Three Saints Bay on Kodiak Island. From the beginning, the Tanaina had the reputation of being powerful, a group to be reckoned with. For fifteen years, the Russians fought many battles with both the Eskimos and the Tanaina Indians in their attempts to establish trading forts. Indians and Eskimos repeatedly attempted to band together to drive out the Russians, but although they won many victories, they were never successful in their main goal.

When the Russians first began to exploit Alaskan fur resources, they did so under the auspices of several private companies. The Shelikov Company was the first and most active of these in southwestern Alaska. (The famous Aleksander Baranov soon took over control of this company at Kodiak.) In 1786, the Lebedev-Lastochkin Company, under Kolomin, arrived in Alaska and established a trading fort among the Tanaina on the Kenai Peninsula at the Kasilof River. At this time there was apparently little conflict between the two companies. For the next five years, both tried to initiate contact with the Indians and Eskimos and to subjugate them. The native peoples were often attacked and their women and children taken to the forts as hostages. Treatment of the hostages did nothing to endear the Russians to the Indians, and repeated attempts to establish a trading fort in the Iliamna area met with only limited success.

In 1791, another party of the Lebedev-Lastochkin Company, under the leadership of Konovalov, entered Cook Inlet and established Fort St. Nicholas (the present village of Kenai). Konovalov immediately attacked both the Shelikov Company and the other contingent of the Lebedev-Lastochkin men, who were led by Kolomin. The Indians also felt Konovalov's wrath. His men went into the Iliamna area, plundering two of the four friendly villages and taking the people into captivity. Frequently, Indians who were found trading with Kolomin or the Shelikov Company were killed and their furs stolen by Konovalov.

For the next few years, brutality, murder, and robbery were common. Those Indians in direct contact with the Russians were reduced to serfdom. During the last ten years of the eighteenth century, the Russian posts were described as virtual harems, the women being conscripted from the surrounding villages. Indians were punished severely for small infractions. Children sent by their parents from distant villages to learn Russian life and manners were forced to help the women hostages perform the manual tasks. Hostilities were ended at last when Baranov, of the Shelikov Company, imprisoned Konovalov. In 1799, the Russian-American Company took over as a monopoly in Alaska, precluding repetition of the Lebedev-Lastochkin problem.

The Tanaina of Iliamna, however, had had enough of the abuses of the Russians. In 1799 they destroyed the fort in their area and killed all the Russians manning it. It was not until about 1821 that the Russians successfully established another trading fort in the Iliamna region.

There are indications that the Tanaina of the Kenai Peninsula objected very early to the encroachment of the Russians on their territory and to the resulting oppressions. In 1786, English traders who sailed into Cook Inlet noticed many deserted houses. The Iliamna Tanaina say that some of their ancestors originally lived in the area but moved inland when they began to feel pressure from the Russians, apparently fleeing as far inland as the Stony River and the Mulchatna River. Later, perhaps after the wealth from the fur trade began to make contact with the Russians more lucrative, they began to filter back nearer the coast to settle in such villages as Kijik and Old Iliamna among the Tanaina who were already there.

After the new fort was established at Iliamna about 1821, the Tanaina began to be drawn more and more into the fur trade. Their involvement continued after the sale of Alaska to the United States and persists, though to a much lesser degree, today.

In 1836, a smallpox epidemic broke out at Sitka and for the next four years spread throughout southwestern Alaska. Indians and Eskimos were severely affected, but it is almost impossible to determine the intensity of the epidemic among the Iliamna Tanaina.

The Russian Orthodox church had attempted some missionization among the Indians since 1794. In 1845, the Kenai mission was established, and missionary work was increased considerably. Priests tried to visit each village in their parish at least once every two years, primarily to perform baptisms and marriages. It is doubtful that much indoctrination into Orthodox Christianity occurred. Orthodoxy seems rather to have become an overlay upon a still viable aboriginal religion.

Records of the Russian Orthodox church show that a Creole (part Russian and part Eskimo or Indian) had taken up residence at Old Iliamna after 1838, apparently in the capacity of lay reader. This man, Savva Rickteroff, was an ancestor of many of the Rickteroffs who are now culturally fully Tanaina and live on Iliamna Lake. Michael Rickteroff, who has been lay reader at Pedro Bay, contributed some of the stories presented here.

Fundamentalist missionaries began to come into the Iliamna area after 1900, and they continue to work there today. Some conflict has occurred occasionally between the fundamentalist and orthodox doctrines.

In 1867, Russia sold Alaska to the United States. The Russian-American Company assets found their way ultimately into the hands of the Alaska Commercial Company, which dealt with the Indians and Eskimos as the former company had. There were several Alaska Commercial Company posts in the Cook Inlet–Iliamna region, which made it possible for the Indians to continue their fur-trading enterprise. A competitor, the Western Fur and Trading Company, also became established in the Cook Inlet area, and the two companies vied with each other for the Indians' trade. Indians were permitted extensive credit on luxury goods as well as hunting and trapping supplies. Because of the competition, fur prices rose, and the Indians enjoyed a period of considerable prosperity. It is said that prices paid the Indians were often on a par with those paid in San Francisco. In 1883, the Alaska Commercial Company bought the Western Fur and Trading Company. Subsequently, fur prices dropped more than 50 per cent without the strong competition to keep them up, and the company cut off credit and tried to collect some of the debts owed by the Indians.

Obviously, the Indians were left destitute. An economic crisis existed throughout southwestern Alaska. In the Iliamna area, private traders helped ease the crisis somewhat by continuing to extend a measure of credit. Prospectors, who began to filter into the Iliamna area during the first ten years of the twentieth century, further supported the staggering economy.

In the late 1800's, salmon canneries were opened. Large fish traps in the rivers, including the Kvichak, which flows from Iliamna, probably reduced greatly the salmon supply to the people of Iliamna Lake. In 1907, however, traps were banned, and the Tanaina are still able to base their subsistence on salmon. About 1915, the Tanaina became involved in the commercial fishing industry in Bristol Bay. After 1940, they began to fish in large sailboats. In 1951, the ban on power boats was removed, and the Tanaina have slowly begun to acquire these for fishing.

The Iliamna Tanaina received their first school in 1905, but it was disbanded in 1926. Another school was opened in 1952, so that children are now able to acquire locally an education through the eighth grade. For high school, they go to one of several boarding schools available in Alaska or other states at the expense of the Bureau of Indian Affairs.

In 1918, the influenza epidemic which affected much of the United States reached southwestern Alaska. Although several villages on the Kvichak River were severely affected, the disease never reached Iliamna in force. The people credit this protection to the exceptional powers of a great shaman.

Today, there are approximately three hundred Tanaina in the Iliamna region. Most of them speak English, although there is some attempt at Nondalton to preserve their own language as well. They are a friendly and enterprising people, and the anthropologist among them is impressed by the absence of the extensive social disorganization which has been the unhappy lot of many other American Indian groups under the overpowering influence of Western civilization.

Culture

Since the culture of any people is constantly changing, a description of their way of life necessarily gives a somewhat static view of what is, in reality, a dynamic and on-going process. This account generally describes the time just prior to contact with Western civilization and the time of cultural elaboration resulting from involvement with the Russian fur trade.

In aboriginal times and until the latter part of the nineteenth century, the Tanaina wore tailored skin clothes. Both men and women wore a garment which could be considered analogous to the long underwear of Western civilization. It was made of dehaired sheepskin or caribou skin, and reached from the neck to halfway between the knees and ankles. For winter, the garment had footwear attached. If it was to be worn while hunting, the hair was left on the skin and turned inside.

Over this basic garment, a skin shirt was worn in summer. The man's shirt reached just above the knees, the woman's, below the knees. After cotton cloth became available through traders, the shirt was often made of this material. In winter, a hooded fur shirt, known in both Eskimo and Indian areas as a parka, was worn. It was pulled over the head because there was no front opening. A caribou-skin coat or a square "poncho" was also used. Knee boots were worn in both summer and winter, the soles made of brown bear or beluga skin, with tops of caribou skin or sheepskin with the hair left on. During rainy weather, a waterproof garment of whale gut was worn, with salmon-skin boots to keep the feet dry. Clothing was decorated with fringes, fur trim, beads, dentalium shells, and porcupine quill work. Decoration often indicated an individual's social rank.

Most of the people of the world practice forms of bodily adornment to enhance beauty as defined by their particular culture. The Tanaina were no exception. They applied black and red face paint to designate clan membership. They inserted labrets into the lower lip, and dentalium shells into holes pierced in the ears and nasal septum. Women's faces were tattooed with lines. Men wore their hair quite long until the end of the nineteenth century. Members of some groups wore a single braid down the back, covered with bird down and feathers. Others wore their hair loose. Women, too, had long hair, which they wore in two braids.

Today, clothing, ornamentation, and hair styles for both men and women conform to the general styles of Western civilization.

Transportation in the North has always been a problem. Thick mosses, brush, and forests make walking difficult in the Alaskan southwest. Many trails existed in the past and some are maintained today, but there are still no roads. The Indians had several methods of making travel easier. In winter, they wore three- to five-foot-long snowshoes made with birch frames and bear or moose babiche webbing. Until after 1900, small one-man sleds were used on the lake ice. A man would sit on the sled and propel himself across the ice with poles. Built-up sleds and dog teams are used today, as in the recent past; but it is not known whether the Tanaina used dog teams with sleds before contact with the Russians. However, dogs have always been kept for hunting and packing.

Rivers and lakes are the highways of the Tanaina. Most travel in summer is by water. Several types of boats have been used. The birchbark canoe was common, especially in interior areas. A moose-skin boat, used to transport game home after hunting trips, was made by stretching the skins over a wood frame. Simple dugout canoes were said to have been made by the Tanaina of Cook Inlet, but there is no record of their having been used in the Iliamna area.

One of the most common crafts of the Tanaina, borrowed from the Eskimo, seems particularly well adapted to a lake and marine environment. This is the *bidarka*, a version of the more northern Eskimo kayak. It was made by stretching sealskin over a spruce frame and came in one-, two-, and three-hole decked-over models. A large nondecked-over model was also made for transporting supplies or numbers of people. This boat is analogous to the Eskimo umiak.

None of these boats is still in use. The Tanaina, as well as their neighbor Eskimos, have adopted instead the wooden skiff with an outboard gasoline motor for lake use. Some of the larger skiffs are also used for fishing in Bristol Bay. A thirty-foot fishing boat with inboard gasoline motor is the preferred craft, however, for safety and for success in fishing.

In the last ten years, the small airplane has become a more common method of transportation in both summer and winter. Several commercial bush pilots operate in the Iliamna area, and recently the younger Tanaina have become interested in flying, some of the more affluent ones having acquired their own small planes.

Because the Tanaina were fortunate enough to live in an environment where game and fish were relatively plentiful, they were able to maintain semisedentary villages with populations of between fifty and two hundred. During the winter months, the people lived in the consolidated villages. Semisubterranean houses, of logs with bark or skin roofs, were occupied by several related families.

Usually the village consisted of four or more of these structures. Compartments built along the sides of the dwellings provided privacy for individual families. A ceremonial or "dance" house was a common feature of a village. Here the villagers entertained guests, played games, and held potlatches. Caches were built above ground on posts for food storage. Fish, however, were usually kept in three-foot-deep holes lined with grass.

During the winter months, food was supplied by hunters, who made excursions into the mountains and killed caribou, bear, and other game animals utilizing spears, sinew-backed bows, and arrows tipped with stone or bone points. The hunters also used deadfalls and surrounds. Dogs assisted by tracking animals, sniffing out bears in hibernation or holding animals at bay. Hunting trips might last for only a day or extend into several weeks. Women often went to the mountains to snare ground squirrels. Regardless of the hunting and trapping activities, the population retained a central, permanent village as its base.

In the early summer, the salmon began to come up the Kvichak River from Bristol Bay into Iliamna Lake and the rivers tributary to it. The people left their winter villages and scattered along the nearby shores of the streams and lake to fish for the salmon. Usually a temporary structure was built which housed only a few persons. A single family with perhaps an older relative or two would inhabit the dwelling. Fishing was done with fish spears at rapids, and with weirs and fish traps. The Tanaina still fish in summer, but use only gill nets now.

Early Russian reports maintain that the Tanaina lived, in summer, in the same structures where their fish were hung. The salmon thus were dried and smoked accidentally by the household fires; thus the fish could be preserved for winter. In more recent times, a separate smokehouse has been used to smoke the fish, and most Indians spend the summer in the ubiquitous white-canvas wall tent that is known throughout the Arctic and sub-Arctic.

The Tanaina also made trips over the portage to Cook Inlet to obtain fish, sea mammals, and clams. Seals were also taken in Iliamna Lake. In the late summer, many varieties of berries ripened, and the Tanaina used them extensively, as well as a number of wild plants. Consequently, the Indians had a varied diet with a minimum of village movement and hardship, unlike some peoples of the interior sub-Arctic who were and are able to maintain only band-sized groups that must move frequently because of scarcity of food.

The Tanaina traded with the neighboring Eskimos and Indians for luxury goods. They traded moose, wolverine skins, porcupine quills, and other items, obtaining in exchange such things as copper arrowheads, cedar arrow shafts, sealskins, and lines. When the Russians came to southwestern Alaska, the Indians extended the already existing concept of trade to include furs.

Cook Inlet was teeming with the sea otter which was so highly valued by the Russians. In the surrounding land, mink, weasel (ermine), beaver, and other valuable fur animals were abundant. By exploiting this resource, some of the Tanaina were able to acquire a level of wealth which was impossible in a strictly aboriginal economy. Successful trappers obtained from the Russians luxury goods such as glass beads, iron, and metal utensils, as well as tea, tobacco, flour, and Russian clothing.

It is noteworthy that guns and ammunition were not traded to the Indians until after the United States purchased Alaska in 1867. Especially adept hunters were permitted to become indebted to the company for luxury goods as well as hunting equipment in exchange for their services.

Today, Tanaina fish commercially in Bristol Bay during the summer to earn cash to buy clothing, some food, and other items of Western manufacture, such as radios, outboard motors, and furniture. Many of the women remain in the village during the summer to catch, smoke, and dry salmon. Men, upon their return home, also supplement the family's diet by hunting game animals and birds.

The social organization of the Tanaina reflects the stability of their population. Clans are relatively rare among people who must live in small bands and move frequently in search of food. With more sedentary and larger populations, however, social elaborations are more likely to occur.

The aboriginal Tanaina traced their descent through the mother's side of the family. The kinship units were extended to include all of the persons related through the mother in matrilineal clans.

The clans owned property as a corporate unit, regulated marriages, and assisted each other when there was a death. The people of nonrelated clans prepared the body and took care of all the arrangements for the funeral. In return, members of the bereaved clan later were hosts at a feast for their helpers, and gifts were given—thus laying the foundation for the later elaborate potlatch. After wealth came into the Tanaina area from the Russian fur trade, potlatches were given to validate a marriage, to establish an individual as an important man, or to help a poor man.

A man in one clan often established a slocin or "blood-brother partnership" with a man of another clan. Through this slocin, social and political contacts were made. When conflicts arose between clans, the slocin was the link through whom peace could be negotiated.

An incipient class system existed in aboriginal times, but when the wealth from the Russian fur trade became abundant, the class system became more crystallized into the "nobility" (rich man, or *cushka*) and the "commoner," or poor man. The commoner relatives of the rich family usually lived in the home of the latter and assisted with work in exchange for support.

Slaves, taken in raids, also became part of the rich man's household, apparently having a status similar to that of the commoner. All were well treated, for it would damage a rich man's position if it became known that he mistreated a slave or poor relative. The Iliamna Tanaina apparently had no "chief." "Rich man" and "chief" were synonymous.

Social control was usually in the hands of the clan. In case of murder or other major crime, it was the duty of the clan members to avenge their wronged member. Public opinion, however, was a powerful force in keeping the community reasonably harmonious and enforcing most of the rules. The rich man often directed public opinion and upheld the status quo.

The culture of a people can be epitomized in the life cycle of the average individual: the major events from birth to death which he experiences.

When a woman became pregnant, she was not allowed to do heavy work but was expected to exercise. A few dietary restrictions were observed, and the woman was not allowed to go near or step over any animal or fish. A special shelter of bark was built for the mother for her delivery, and a midwife assisted with the birth. The placenta was tied to a young spruce tree in the woods so that the child would grow straight and tall as the young tree. The mother drank juice from a boiled plant to help her body heal. The child was kept in a birchbark cradle, and tundra moss was placed in the bottom of it for a diaper. The decorated skin of an unborn animal was the infant's clothing.

Adoption used to be fairly common. If a family had too many children to care for adequately, or if the mother died, the child was usually given to a relative and treated as a member of that family. Children were wanted and cared for. Not only did they assist with the work when they were young, but they supported their aging parents in later years. Tanaina are permissive parents who rarely resort to corporal punishment. If a child is behaving badly, he will be talked to or given some additional chore.

Today, as in the past, the child helps with tasks around the home by the age of eight or ten. Boys go hunting and fishing with their fathers; girls assist with the preparation of the fish and cook and sew. Children of both sexes were and are permitted to play together, although by about ten years of age they tend to separate into play groups of one sex. Children and adolescents of both sexes and different ages, however, often participate in sports and parties together.

In the past, a girl was confined at puberty to special quarters for a year, where she was taught the things a woman should know, including sewing, cooking, and correct behavior. A boy had no special puberty rite. When he killed his first fish or animal, however, there would be a ceremony and the older people would eat the game. The mother's brother was often active in training the boy in hunting and other masculine activities. Today there are no special puberty observances for either boys or girls.

In aboriginal times, marriage was simple. A boy moved into the home of the girl's parents and began to assist them. Occasionally, the couple would move to the home of the boy's parents after a one- to five-year residence with the girl's parents. An individual was required to marry someone outside his own clan, but he was permitted to choose the person either from his own village or from another.

After the Russian fur trade began to place more wealth in the hands of the men, a man frequently obtained a woman by paying a bride price rather than performing bride service for her. A potlatch validating the marriage was also required. In this ceremony, goods and food were given away to members of other clans. The more wealthy and important the man, the more impressive was the potlatch. Polygyny was permitted, but only a wealthy man could afford more than one wife. Today, marriages are arranged much as in Western civilization and are formalized in church.

When a person lay dying, the family made loud noises to frighten away evil spirits. After death, as was mentioned earlier, members of another clan prepared the body.

Before disposal of the body, ceremonial mourning took place. The head of the house blackened his face, placed an eagle feather in his nasal septum, and wore an eagle feather headdress. He led the mourning, ringing a bell, contorting his body, moaning, and eulogizing the dead in a song. Other mourners improvised song stanzas which were sung to the beating of drums.

One year after his death a potlatch was held in honor of the deceased.

In aboriginal times, the body was cremated. Then the bones were collected in a box and placed in a "cemetery." After the Russians came to Alaska, the pattern changed to burial. Small houses or boxes were placed over the grave of the deceased person, and gifts of food, clothing, or utensils were often left for him. Now a fence, at least, usually encircles each grave, at the head of which is commonly placed a Russian Orthodox cross.

It was believed in the past that the dead lived in the interior of the earth where there was twilight. When the living were awake, they slept; when the dead were awake, the living slept.

The shaman (or sorcerer or medicine man, as he is often called) was an important member of the community. He might also be a rich man, but he was always a leader. He was said to receive his power through dreams whether he wished it or not. There were "little" shamans with limited power, and powerful shamans who could do spectacular acts of magic or curing. Some of the shamans were "good," but others were "bad." The bad ones always tried to bring harm, and the good ones attempted to counteract it.

A shaman could be either male or female, but the male appears to have been more significant. He had elaborate paraphernalia. His parka was the typical Tanaina one with added appendages of claws and beaks that rattled when he danced. He acted as priest, magician, and medical practitioner. When a person was sick, the shaman would be called to cure him. He had a doll which apparently acted as a "familiar." During the ceremony, the room was darkened and the shaman danced to the rhythm of drumming, holding the doll. At the climax, he thrust the doll at the sick person, and the doll disappeared. The shaman collapsed from exhaustion. The next night the dance was repeated, and at its climax the shaman withdrew the doll, which had been inside the sick person's body attempting to expel the evil force causing the illness.

Another method of curing was by "sucking." Illness could be caused by an intrusive object sent by a bad shaman. By sucking the painful area, the shaman could remove the object and thus cure the illness.

Shamans were supposed to be able to travel in their dreams. It was believed that they had powerful animal "familiars." A shaman could change himself into his animal, the better to accomplish a task. If the "familiar" died, however, the shaman would also die.

Shamans sometimes put on public displays to impress the people with their powers, including competitions among themselves to gain status. Some are said to have been able to fly through the air at great speeds and make objects appear or disappear. One shaman was credited with preventing the 1918 influenza epidemic from reaching the Iliamna villages.

Shamanistic practices have dwindled considerably during the twentieth century, but I believe the art is still practiced to some extent. Being a shaman does not preclude being a devout Christian. On the contrary, at the beginning of the twentieth century, some of the more active church members were practicing shamans. Christianity and shamanism need not be mutually exclusive. The belief in the spirit of God, holy water, the mystical power of the church, and other Christian elements can be incorporated easily into shamanism.

The Tanaina believed in spirits. There were giants who lived in the forest, and many folk tales are woven around these beings. They might come and take food or steal individuals from the villages, and so were a force to be feared. Offerings were made for luck at a large rock on the trail over the portage to Cook Inlet, where imprints were found of a giant who had passed there searching for his sister. Offerings were thrown in the water near a point where a shaman was buried.

Animals play a major part in the belief system. The raven, or *chulyen*, is supposed to have created the world and people. The loon, one of the shaman's birds, often warns when a storm is coming. A wolf is considered a "brother." If a person were hungry in the forest, the wolf would bring him food.

In cultures which possess no writing system, folk tales preserve the traditions of the people. The oral tradition includes stories which recount history, explain the origin of the earth and the peoples and animals on it, and instruct the people in the moral precepts of the culture. Other series of stories may be told mainly for pleasure. The collection presented here is primarily for entertainment, although the reader may perceive some elements of instruction in what is right or wrong, good or bad, according to Tanaina values.

Some elements in the stories certainly are results of contact with Western civilization. Many embellishments, particularly those which incorporate the *cushka* concept, may have been acquired during the period of economic and social elaboration after the fur trade was instituted, and grafted onto older story motifs. That the stories are basically aboriginal Tanaina rather than European, however, cannot be denied. Motifs in the stories are those common to the folklore of many American Indian groups, particularly the Athapascans.

The raven (*chulyen*) stories are particularly interesting in their relationship with the mythology of other American Indian groups. *Chulyen* is the Tanaina version of the ubiquitous Trickster—an ambiguous, mischievous figure who often breaks the taboos of a society and behaves contrary to the value system. He is at once a hero and a clown, a creator and a destroyer. Paul Radin has provided a classic study of the Trickster, particularly as he is found among the Winnebago Indians. The animal cast in the role of Trickster varies from one Indian group to another. He may be a spider, a coyote, or a hare. Close relatives of the Tanaina, such as the Tanana and Tlingit, consider him a raven.

These two societies also have Trickster cycles very similar to those of the Tanaina.

The neighboring Athapascan, Tlingit, and Haida peoples use many of the motifs of the other stories presented here, and they often retain whole stories which are similar.

Underlying all these stories, then, there is the foundation of an old and common Athapascan oral tradition.

JOAN B. TOWNSEND

University of Manitoba

Tanaina Tales from Alaska

When the legends die, the dreams end.

When the dreams end, there is no more greatness.

HAL BORLAND,
When the Legends Die

The Chickadee Story

THERE WAS ONCE A LITTLE *skaga*, or chickadee, who was really cranky. He just couldn't get along with anyone. He often went out of his way to cause trouble for someone when it would have been much easier to be friendly.

He was walking along the beach one day when he came across a *nikaseenithulooyee*, or something like an alligator, lying at the water's edge. It was half in and half out of the water. The little chickadee right away ran over and jumped on the alligator's back and began running up and down it.

This bothered the alligator.

"Hey!" he said. "You get off my back!"

The chickadee was stubborn, though, and wouldn't get off. He just kept running up and down.

The alligator was getting madder.

"You better get off of my back," he said.

The chickadee was pretty cranky, though, and he said, "You better shut up, or I'll kick your ribs in."

By this time the alligator was furious. He reached up, and before the chickadee could blink, snapped one of his legs off and threw him up on the beach.

The chickadee got up and limped way back off the beach away from the alligator. Then he sat down and spliced a piece of grass onto his leg. After he'd pouted for a while, he walked back on down along the shoreline.

By this time he was getting pretty thirsty from losing so much blood, but of course he couldn't drink the ocean water (it was too salty), so he went back inland to look for some lakes.

Before long he found two big ones side by side. He went to the first lake and drank it completely dry. Then he staggered over and drained the other one.

By this time his stomach was so big he could hardly move. When he tried to walk, he fell over on his back and couldn't get up. He felt pretty bad. But he knew there was a village nearby, so he started singing:

> *"yu nuk' no   tu no sho je lay tosh'*
> *hina no wush   lok'nay"*

(You people up there. Come down here and bring me up. I want to be your kind, or be one of you.)

Skaga was crying and singing at the same time, to make the villagers feel sorry for him.

Finally they heard him and came running down. Someone fetched a reindeer hide to pack him up to the *gazhee*. But when they set it down beside the cranky chickadee, he said, "No! It's not big enough!"

He was just a little feller, but he thought he was a big man.

So the people ran back up to the village and brought down a bear skin. But the chickadee was too ornery.

"No!" he said. "It's still not big enough!"

So they made one more trip back up to the village and brought down the skin of a mouse.

4

"Ah!" said the chickadee. "That's just right!"

He stretched out on the mouse hide and they carried him up the hill to the *gazhee*. But just as they were about to carry him through the door, he said, "Wait! Don't carry me through that door. It's too small."

When they asked him how they could get him inside, he said, "You'll have to put me through the eye of a needle."

So one of the villagers went inside to find a bone needle. When he came back out, he had one with a big eye in it. But the chickadee scowled and said, "It's not big enough."

Someone groaned, and several others ran around trying to find a bigger needle. Finally, after much searching, they came back with the biggest one in the village. The eye was huge.

"It's still not big enough," the chickadee snapped.

Then a real old woman stepped out from the others. She was the grandma of the whole village and very wise. She pulled out a tiny needle with a wee small eye. You could just barely see it on a bright day.

"It's just right," said the chickadee.

So they held the tiny needle right up in front of the door and pushed the little bird through it. He fell with a plop! on the *gazhee* floor.

The villagers soon found that the chickadee was just as ornery inside as outside. They fed him, and tried to be nice to him, but he was just as mean as he could be.

"Lay me over next to the fire," he said.

So they did. But he kept on bossing them until one villager got so mad he picked up a piece of white granite and tossed it into the fire. When the Indians build steam baths, they pack rocks around the sides of the fire. Then, when the rocks get red-hot, they pour water on them to make steam. But they never use white granite, because it cracks when heated and sometimes even explodes.

This villager knew that.

Whang! It exploded, and one chip shot right through the chickadee's stomach, which was still bloated from all the drinking he'd done, and out gushed all the water.

It flooded so fast that nobody had a chance to escape. Everyone was swimming for his life inside the *gazhee*—even the chickadee. But still the water rushed out until the house was completely filled.

Just then the old grandma spotted a huge clam shell floating by, so she climbed onto it and paddled out the door with her hands. She was the only one to escape from the *gazhee* alive.

As the water ebbed away, the old lady just kept paddling around. Finally everything went dry, and her clam shell came to rest on solid ground. The only thing left standing in the village was her *nichithl*. Everything else had washed away with the flood.

So old Grandma got off her shell boat and went inside to build a fire. Later, when she had a good hot fire going, she went back outside to look around. She hadn't gone far when she spotted the chickadee's body right over where the *gazhee* had stood. So she picked it up and carried it back to her *nichithl*.

Inside, the old lady set to work cleaning and skinning the dead chickadee. Then, after she put the meat to roast over the fire, she rendered out the fat. When the oil had cooled, she poured it into a tiny mouse stomach and hung it up above her bed. She would save that for special occasions.

Soon the chickadee roasts were done, and the old lady had her supper. Then she cleaned up and turned in for the night.

Directly above her hung the tiny mouse stomach filled with chickadee oil.

That evening the wind picked up. It blew so hard that branches were torn from trees. But the old grandma slept on, refusing to be waked up.

While she slept the wind blew an *alutika,* or spruce needle, in through the door of the *nichithl,* and it pierced the mouse stomach, causing the chickadee oil to trickle out. Running down the sides of the little sack, it dripped from the bottom straight into the old lady's eyes. She awoke with a start.

"I'm blind!" she cried. But there was no one to hear. The oil seared and burned its way deep into her eyes until eventually she died, in very great pain.

The Mouse Story
(The Rich Man's Son)

ONCE THERE WAS a rich man's son who was unbelievably lazy. This *cushkaveah* never did any more than he was forced to do. He just refused to work. In falltime, when all the villagers pitched in to put up fish for the winter, he wouldn't lift a finger. He was spoiled because his father was the rich man, or chief, of the village, and had slaves captured from other tribes to do most of the work around their house.

One time when his mother absolutely forced him to work a little, he got his whole village in trouble. She'd been boiling fish inside their *nichithl* and had told him to keep spooning the foam off as it formed on the surface of the water. (Even if salmon are scrubbed down before cooking, as they boil a sudsy scum which must be scraped off forms on top of the water. It is gurry from the outside of the fish and is sometimes poisonous.)

As he was spooning off the foam, the rich man's son saw a mouse running across the floor. So he scooped up a large spoonful of the boiling water and threw it at the tiny animal, who squeaked with pain and ran out the door badly burned.

The rich man's son didn't think much about what he'd done, so he never mentioned it to any of the other villagers, and it was lucky for him that he didn't. For the people were very superstitious about certain things in those days. For instance, they would never brag about how much food they had or how easy life was. And they were careful not to injure little animals. They had more respect for mice, mountain squirrels, shrews, etc., than we do today, because they figured the little animals were people to one another. The old-timers believed that mice look at other mice just as we look at other people, and that these little folk have certain powers over the lives of humans. The people were afraid that if they broke any of these taboos, hard times would come and game would get scarce. But the young man paid no attention to these things—or to the older people—and nothing was said.

Leaves began dropping from the trees as the nights turned colder, and the slaves hurried to put up the last of the fish before freeze-up. Fall passed and winter came on hard. With the first snows the village hunters were out day and night looking for signs of game, but there weren't any to be found. They drove far back into the mountains with their mixed-breed dog teams to places beyond their usual hunting grounds, but there wasn't any game.

Things were getting desperate at the village as the people started using up the last of the fish. Many were forced to kill off their dogs, for they couldn't afford to feed them any longer. They were having to eat the dogs' flesh themselves.

When they got down to nothing, it began to storm. It was snowing and drifting and blowing for days on end, and then it turned bitter cold. By this time the people were starving. They had been on strict rations for some time, but now the last of everything was gone. No one had the strength to go out and cut wood. They were so weak they couldn't get out of their beds.

Even the rich man's son was getting weak—although he wasn't so bad off as the rest, because he'd been sneaking a little above his ration at nights. But, as the end came in sight, he thought of what he'd done that summer, and he knew that the famine was his fault.

With the little strength he had left, he slipped on his clothes and went off into the woods packing his bow and arrows. He walked and walked and walked through the timbers until he found a *kon*, or colony of mice. Even through the storm he could see all the little mouse holes in the frozen moss and trails in the snow.

Then he heard a woman's voice.

"Shut your eyes," it said. "Put your sleeve over your face, and walk around the colony three times in the same direction that the sun moves. Then put your head down against the ground."

The rich man's son was afraid, but he did as he was told, and when he laid his head against the ground . . . BANG! . . . he fell right into a house. When he opened his eyes he was on the floor of a small room, and there was a woman close by him sitting in a chair. She looked just like any other woman, and a fire was burning softly in the center of the room. She offered him a chair.

"I know your village is starving," the woman said. "I'm the one who made you come here." She had a kind voice. "Do you remember doing anything this past summer that you shouldn't have done?" she asked him.

The rich man's son thought for a moment. Then he remembered the mouse. He felt very bad about it, but he admitted to her that he'd poured boiling water on a little mouse.

"Yes," she said. "That's right. You burned my little baby pretty badly." The woman stood up and he followed her over to a small room set apart by a blanket. She drew the cover aside,

10

and there was her little baby. He was crusted with scars and blisters.

"That's why you people are starving," she said. "I've always told the little ones never to run away from home, but this one wouldn't mind, and ran down to your village."

For the first time in his life the rich man's son felt really bad. He was ashamed of what he'd done, and he honestly told her how sorry he was.

The woman could see that he was being truthful, so she invited him to sit up and have supper with her. Afterward, she spoke to him again.

"You can go back to the village now," she said, "and things will be all right. Just be sure you never harm any little ones again."

She told him to leave the same way he'd come. "Close your eyes and put your sleeve over your face, then put your head against the door."

He did, and when he opened his eyes, he was outside again—standing in the same place as before. When he looked around there was no house in sight—only the mouse holes.

So he picked up his bow and arrows and started walking back toward the village, feeling stronger after that good meal. Not far from home he heard sounds ahead of him on the trail. So he sneaked along through the timber until he spotted what made the noise—a herd of caribou! He got right in close, then jumped up and started shooting with his bow and arrow. He killed about a dozen.

He cut one open and carried the heart and liver back to his people. They were still too weak to help themselves, so he cut wood and cooked for them. For the first time in his life he really worked—and he found that he didn't mind it at all.

When the meat was done, he gave each a spoonful. He knew they shouldn't eat too much all at once after being starved for so long. Gradually, then, as time passed, he increased their ration, until a few of the men were strong enough to go help him pack the rest of the meat in.

So life returned to normal in the village, and from then on the rich man's son was the hardest worker of them all. And never again was he to injure one of the little people. He'd learned his lesson.

The Porcupine
and the Beaver

THE PORCUPINE AND BEAVER used to be traveling companions.
They were good friends and even lived together. But when they
ate, the porcupine climbed up into birch trees to eat the bark,
and the beaver crawled in among the brushes on his belly eating
willows. The porcupine could climb all around in trees, but the
beaver couldn't, so the porcupine always made fun of him.

"Come on up and climb like me."

"I can't."

The porcupine laughed.

"You know why," he said. "It's because you've got such a big
flat tail. It's always in your way. My tail is small. You always
think that you're better than me, but you can't climb trees."

Actually, the porcupine was jealous of the beaver. It was an
old Indian custom to wash and clean the bones of certain animals
and throw them back in the water. They believed that if the
bones weren't broken the animal would come back to life. So
they were always careful with the bones of beavers and wolver-

13

ines and certain other animals. But they didn't bother about porcupines. That was why the porcupine was jealous of the beaver.

"You're so particular about having your bones washed and cleaned," he said. "Not me. You're too particular."

This really made the beaver mad.

Later on they were crossing a stream, and the porcupine had to ride on the beaver's back. The beaver started splashing water all over him and tried to shake him off. He shook and shook, but the porcupine hung on. They rubbed together so much that they rubbed all the fat off the beaver's back and the porcupine's stomach, and neither one has ever got it back.

Finally the porcupine fell off into the water and splashed his way to shore. The beaver laughed and made fun of him.

"You go climb trees," he said. "I'll stick to the water."

The Loon Story

THERE WAS AN OLD BLIND MAN in the village who had a wife and one son. They had to lead him around everywhere he went. He could see a little outside on a bright day, but not inside or in the dark.

One morning he said to his wife, "Let's go into the woods and hunt. Maybe you'll get a spruce chicken or something."

Game was scarce and they had to go a long way from the village. After a three-day trip the family made camp in some flat country far from home.

Unknown to the rest of the village, the woman had been starving her husband for a long time. Many of the people had been giving her what food they could spare, because they knew her husband couldn't hunt any more and they respected him. However, the old man never got any of the food. She cooked it for herself and the boy, and threw her husband the bones. Since he was blind, he never knew. He just figured that times were hard and food was scarce.

One day while they were in camp his wife said to him, "Let's go for a walk in the woods."

"You know I'm blind," he said. "How can I walk in the woods, when I can't see?"

"We'll guide you," she said.

So they walked out of their little camp and hiked way off into the woods. By and by she told him to sit down on a stump to rest.

"Let's leave your daddy there for a while," she whispered to the little boy. "We'll come back for him after he's rested."

Then she took the boy and started for home.

After a while the old man began to suspect that she had abandoned him. He was hungry, so he took out some dry fish eggs that he had in his pocket and ate them. That filled him up, but now he was thirsty. He couldn't see anything, so he got down on his hands and knees and began crawling along the ground in search of water.

He didn't know how long he crawled, because he couldn't tell the difference between night and day, but he was terribly tired and hungry and thirsty, and it was cold and damp on the ground. Once he thought he could see daylight.

When his thirst was getting so bad he thought he would die the old man heard a loon. So he turned and began crawling in the direction of the sound. Soon he felt stones under him like on a beach, and at last he came to water. As he put his face down into the water and began drinking, he felt ripples on the surface and knew that the loon was coming toward him. He finished drinking and waited. Finally, the loon came near him on the beach, and as it stepped out of the water it turned into a man.

"What's the trouble?" he asked the blind old-timer.

So the old man told him his story.

"Here," said the loon-man coming closer. "Put your head under my arm."

As the old man did this, the loon jumped back into the lake

and began swimming around. When he had circled it three times he dived underwater, pulling the old man down with him.

When they came up, the loon let go of him and said, "Now, open your eyes and take a look."

"I can see," said the old man. "But not good."

So the loon did the same thing again. He swam around the lake two or three times with the old man under his arm, then dived. When they surfaced that time, the old man could see clearly.

"What should I do now?" he asked.

"Take your little boy and leave your wife," was the answer.

"Well," said the old-timer, "I feel sorry for her, but I guess she doesn't feel sorry for me."

So he thanked the loon and headed back for camp. Just before he got there he stopped and whittled out a birch cane. Then he stumbled into camp pretending that he still couldn't see.

When the little boy saw him coming, he was happy and ran to meet him. But the wife was irritated and wondered how he ever found his way home.

"I'm thirsty," said the old man. "Give me a drink of water."

His wife went to fetch him water out of an old stagnant basin full of bugs. When she brought him a cup, however, he looked at it and said, "Here! I'd like to see you drink this."

His wife was stunned. "How did you know?" she asked.

"I can see just as good as you can now," he said.

She was really mad, but the boy was happy over it.

"Do you want to stay with your mother?" the old man asked him. "Or would you rather come along with me?"

The boy wanted to go with his father, so the two of them headed back to the village together.

When they arrived, the people wondered how he got back his sight, so he told his story to them, and they were all happy for him and angry with the wife.

Later, when she came back to the village complaining because

17

he had thrown her out, nobody felt sorry for her, and from then on she didn't get along very well with the people.

The old man and his boy were always happy, however, and both of them made it a point never to shoot loons after that.

The Lynx
and the Wolverine

A LONG TIME AGO the lynx and wolverine used to be traveling companions and good friends. One day they found a cache.

"I wonder what's in that cache," said the wolverine.

"I don't know," said the lynx. "Must be something."

The wolverine tried to climb up to the cache, but he couldn't make it, so the lynx jumped up onto the platform and opened the door.

"There's lots of meat up here," he said.

He dropped a rawhide rope down over the side and the wolverine pulled himself up. Then the two of them began eating.

"I think I hear somebody talking," said the lynx.

"Oh, you're always hearing things."

"No, I really hear someone."

"It's just the wind," said the wolverine, tearing at a scrap of meat. "Sometimes the wind sounds like people talking."

Then they heard a man's voice saying, "There *is* someone in the cache."

19

The lynx looked through the door and saw two boys coming, so he leaped out and ran off.

"Look," said one of the boys. "There goes *Kashna* [spotted-tail]."

When the lynx got into the woods he stopped and sat down.

"I wonder why they called me that!"

Then he looked down and saw the black spot on the tip of his tail.

"Oh!" he said. "That's why."

He waited there for the wolverine, but his friend didn't come.

Late that night the lynx returned to the cache. The boys had killed the wolverine and skinned him out. He was sitting there propped up against the cache with his mouth open, smiling.

"*Edah* [pal]," called the lynx. "I see you smiling."

But the wolverine didn't answer because he was dead.

So that same night the lynx sneaked into the boys' village and found the wolverine's skin where they had it all stretched out. Without making any noise he stole it and ran back to the cache. When he got to the wolverine's body he stretched the skin over it and his friend came back to life.

Then they started off again through the woods.

A little while later as they were walking along the trail they came to a deadfall. *Edashla* was in the lead, and when he bent over to go under it, he walked straight into a snare and was killed.

Just then the lynx heard the trappers coming, so he ran off.

Right behind him several men from the village walked up and found the dead wolverine. They were happy to see that, and took the snare off him and packed him home. Everyone there was glad.

"*Edah*," they said. "We're sure glad to see you."

They dressed him all up like a king and brought gifts to him. The villagers always used to do this to make fun of *Edashla*. Then they took everything back and skinned him out. They cut the meat all up and cooked and ate the wolverine. Afterward, they gathered up all the bones in one bunch and threw them away. They believed that he would come back to life if they did that.

And he did come back to life, and went looking for his pal. The lynx saw him coming.

"*Edashla*! I thought you were dead."

"You know they can't kill me," the wolverine said.

That made the lynx angry.

"I wonder why they call you 'pal,' " he said. "You always steal from them and eat their food, and yet they can't kill you. They even give you gifts and make you king."

So they got into an argument and split up after that. Now they never hang around together. Wherever there are lots of wolverines there won't be many lynx, and where there are lots of lynx there won't be many wolverines.

First Beaver Story

A MAN WAS WALKING along a riverbank one morning. He had walked for several days already when he saw someone up ahead of him. It was a woman picking gum off trees and chewing it and eating it.

He tried to keep her from seeing him, but as he sneaked closer she looked up and saw him.

"Hey," she said.

He asked her what she was doing.

"Eating gum."

"You like that?"

"Yes."

He said, "Give me your knife and I'll pick the gum for you." She was very pretty.

He cut and picked gum all day for her. She especially liked the gum that turns white when you eat it.

At the end of the day he said, "Come home with me and see my little house."

22

She went home with him and they slept. The next day he got up and fixed something for breakfast—lots of meat. But she wouldn't eat that. Instead, she walked out into the woods and ate brushes. They were waist high with small leaves and looked like willows or alders, but they tasted like sugar cane.

The man worked hard all morning. At noon, he said, "I'll fix lunch."

He cooked up all kinds of meats. Thick and lean. Greasy and fat and juicy. Then he spooned it out onto their wooden plates. But the woman said, "I don't like that stuff. I can't eat it."

So she ran out and packed in some brush.

"I eat this," she said. "Here, try it."

He did, and liked it very much. It tasted like sugar.

"That's all I like," she said.

And he said, "Well, there's lots of that around."

So he went out and cut up an armload of brush and brought it in to her. They both ate it.

Later that day he cooked meat and ate supper.

The woman stayed with him all fall. But she kept going off and getting lost in the woods. She'd go out every morning, then when she came back, her hair would be all wet. He had a hard time keeping track of her.

Finally one day she wandered off and didn't come back. When he went out to look around he found her swimming with some beavers in a lake. She didn't see him though. He went back home and waited for her.

"Did you have a good time?" he asked when she came back.

"Yes," she said. Then she suspected that he knew, so she told him.

"You know what you fellas call beaver? That's what I am."

She just told him right out.

He said, "That's all right."

After that he used to go and swim with her and the rest of the

23

beavers sometimes. But he couldn't stand it very long. It was too cold.

One day she said to him, "You know how to make fire?"

"Yes."

"So do beavers." And she gave him power to stay warm in water.

Every fall he used to go home and visit his people, so one time in September-month he told her he was leaving. First he helped her gather a winter's food supply (threw it on the bank where she could get it), then he went back to the village.

The people there all knew he was staying with a beaver-woman.

They asked him, "Where is the woman that was staying with you?"

He said, "I don't know."

He was ashamed of her. But they told him they knew and asked lots of questions.

"How do you talk to her?" And on and on.

He stayed in the village all winter, but the next fall he went back to his *nichithl.*

The fire was going. She was in there cooking meat for him. She had lots of little beavers. She told him they were his.

The little ones were just like her, and turned into people. But when they went swimming they turned back into beavers. They made a good family, because they didn't eat anything but brush which was cheap food.

Sometimes, the man's friends came to visit him. When she was out of the house they asked him where she came from.

He said, "That's my wife."

"How's come she never eats in front of anyone?"

When she couldn't hear, he said, "She's a beaver-woman."

Then one day when no one was around she said, "Come with me." So he followed her to a small beaver pond.

She turned to him. "Come dive with me. I'll show you the inside of my beaver house."

"I don't think I can stay under water that long."

"Put your head under my arm," she said.

So he did, and she dived under with him and came up inside the beaver house. It was big, but he didn't know how he could get out.

She turned into a beaver.

Later on she took off her coat and turned back into a woman.

Once in a while she would go out to get food—brushes and meat. She made fire by saying strange words and making motions with her hands.

The man stayed quite a while, but he wasn't satisfied and wanted to go.

Then one day the next fall, she said, "Put your head under my arm."

He did, and she brought him back out into the lake. When they crawled up onto the shore she said, "You can go home now."

But he said, "I don't want to. I enjoy staying here. I like just eating and swimming around."

So she did something to him and he changed into a beaver.

They lived there all the time after that. Sometimes they would change into people, but mostly they just stayed beavers.

Second Beaver Story

A LONG TIME AGO two mean, cranky uncles took their lazy nephew beaver-hunting in the old style. They chopped a hole in the top of the beaver house and put him down in it to watch for beavers coming up. Then they went and waited at the two doors. The sound of the chopping had scared the beavers away, but they would come back to the house sooner or later.

However, after they had watched a long while and nothing had happened, the two uncles decided to leave. So they went back to the hole in the roof where they found their lazy nephew asleep.

One of the uncles said, "Such a nephew is not worth having."

The other agreed, so together they patched the top back over and left the boy in it to die.

Late that night when he woke up cold and hungry the nephew knew what had happened and he was afraid.

Just then two big beavers came up out of the water into the house. They started talking to each other:

26

"There's a lost man. He's cold and hungry."

One of the beavers came up to the nephew and began talking to him.

"They left you here to die because you're lazy and sleep all the time," the beaver told him. "But now you'll be better than them."

They started a fire. Then they killed and cooked up one of their slaves and fed him to the abandoned nephew.

They put another slave to work cutting a hole in the roof.

When it was finished he thanked them and started to leave.

"You will be a mighty hunter now," they told him.

But he promised them he would never hunt beavers again. Then he got out and went home.

When he arrived back at the village, he really scared the people—especially the cranky old uncles—because he wouldn't tell them how he got out of the beaver house.

As time went by people discovered that he was not a lazy nephew any longer either. He was a hard worker and a mighty hunter.

But no one ever knew why it was that he refused to hunt beavers again until the day he died.

The Crow Story
(Chulyen)

AFTER THE GIANT of Lake Iliamna lost his sister he built a large canoe. He had walked around for months looking for her without any luck, so he built the canoe figuring he could cover more distance by water.

Since he lived by himself, there was no one else around to admire his craft—that is until old *Chulyen*, the crow, flew over one day. When *Chulyen* saw the canoe down there on the beach he almost came to a dead stop in mid-air. He circled several times until a plan formed in his mind; then he flew on out of sight and landed in the woods.

Now old *Chulyen* had a very strong mind and whenever he needed a disguise he could change himself into a man or whatever he wanted. So now he thought real hard, "I wish I were a man. Make me a handsome prince—a rich man's son."

So he was changed into a young handsome man with fine clothes and a nice moustache, and he walked out of the forest to meet the giant. *Chulyen* walked right up to him and started

28

talking. The giant seemed to like the young man, so it wasn't long before the subject swung around to the canoe.

"It's sure a fine canoe," *Chulyen* said politely. "Do you suppose it would be all right if I tried it out a little bit—just right here in the bay, I mean? You wouldn't mind, would you?"

"Not at all," replied the giant. He was pleased that such a nice young man admired his canoe so much.

So old *Chulyen* pushed the canoe out from the beach and paddled around in a circle, not very far offshore. Then he brought the canoe back and thanked the giant for the ride.

"That's quite all right. Any time," the giant said. "Any time at all."

So the next day the young man came back again, to talk with the giant and take a ride in his canoe. Only this time when he took it, *Chulyen* paddled quite a bit farther out in the bay— almost to the mouth—before he turned around and brought the canoe back. Again he thanked the giant for the ride.

"Any time," the giant said.

It was early in the morning of the third day when the young man showed up for another ride. By this time the giant really liked him and trusted him with the canoe. He smiled as he pushed old *Chulyen* out in the water and watched him paddle around in the bay, then clear out and around the point and out of sight. He stood there on the beach for quite a while waiting for the young man to bring his canoe back, before he realized that he wasn't coming back.

Meanwhile, old *Chulyen* was really laughing at how he had fooled the silly giant, and tricked him out of such a fine canoe. He paddled around all day just enjoying himself, and when night came he camped many miles from the home of the giant.

The next morning he got up and spent the whole day just paddling by himself in the canoe. But by the end of the third afternoon he began to get lonely. He decided it wasn't much fun paddling around by himself. So he started looking for a

partner. As he paddled along the beach, he began singing this
song:

"*Vud sha dah' ga yu' a*" or "Who wants to come along with me
for a ride?"

Before long a moose heard him singing and walked out on the
beach.

"How about me?" he asked. "I'd like to go along with you for
a ride."

"Oh, not you!" said the young man. "Your hooves are too
sharp. They might make a hole in the bottom of my canoe. No,
I don't want *you* for a partner."

A porcupine came out next, and said:

"How about me? I'd like to come out and go for a ride with
you."

"No. Not you," said old *Chulyen*. "Your quills are too sharp.
They might make holes in the sides of my canoe."

Pretty soon then a nice fat seal popped up alongside the canoe
and said, "How about taking me for a partner? I'd like to ride
in your canoe."

"You're just the one I want," said the crow. "Come on and
get in."

As the seal climbed into the boat he looked so fat and juicy
that the old crow started thinking right away how to kill him
and eat him.

Chulyen told the seal that it was getting late and they'd better
stop and make camp. He said he knew of a good spot. So they
went ashore and pulled the canoe up out of the water. Then old
Chulyen turned back into a crow and started walking up into
the woods with the seal following along behind. He was heading
for a place he remembered far inland where there wasn't any
water. The crow knew that the seal couldn't survive for very
long without water. Old *Chulyen* was pretty wise and very
crooked.

When they finally reached the spot they made camp, and the

crafty old crow sat down next to the fire.

"What are we going to eat," he asked. "I'm hungry."

"I don't know," said the seal. "I'm getting hungry too."

The crow thought for a while. Then he said:

"I know what we can do. I'll cut my foot off and roast it on a stick for you over the fire, and you can cut off one of your flippers and cook it for me."

But the seal said, "I don't want to do that. It'll hurt too much."

"No, no," said *Chulyen*, "it won't hurt. You watch. I'll make it so you won't even feel it."

And before the seal could say another word the crow grabbed an ax and chopped off one of his flippers. Then quickly he spit on the wound and rubbed it all over.

"Why it doesn't hurt at all," said the seal.

As they watched, the seal's wound healed right over.

"See," said the crow, "I told you."

Then he whacked off his own skinny foot for the seal. Soon they were both sizzling over the fire. But the seal began to feel that he'd been cheated. As the crow's foot cooked, it shriveled up and turned hard and black, and didn't look very good to eat at all. But the seal's flipper was roasting a juicy brown and grease was just rolling off the sides, making sizzling sounds as it sputtered in the fire.

The seal remarked how dried up and skinny the crow's foot was, while his own flipper was fat and greasy, and that the trade didn't seem quite fair. So as soon as the seal turned his back the crow smeared grease from the flipper all over his foot, which by that time looked like a burnt stick.

"Look," he said. "Grease is coming out all over my foot now."

The seal looked, and sure enough, real grease was rolling liberally down the grizzled remains of *Chulyen's* spindly foot. He felt a little better.

Soon the meat was done, and the two partners settled back for

31

a feast. The seal's flipper tasted excellent, and made a meal fit for a chief, but the crow's foot tasted even worse than it looked. The only thing it did was make the seal thirsty.

"I need a drink," he said. "That dried-up foot made me thirsty. Where can I find some water?"

"You wait right here," said *Chulyen*. "I'll go look for water. When I find some I'll bring it back here for you."

The seal thought it was nice of the crow to make such an offer and said, yes, that would be fine. So old *Chulyen* went off to search for water.

For the longest time, however, he didn't even leave camp. He just hung around in the bushes and watched the blubbery seal get thirstier and thirstier. Then, when the old crow *did* leave, he stayed away for quite a while. By the time he finally came strolling back into camp with some water the seal thought he was going to die and ran to meet him. But just before they reached each other the crow tripped and fell and spilled the water all over the ground. The seal almost had a heart attack.

Chulyen apologized so much the fainting seal forgave him. Then he said, "Come on with me. I'll show you where you can get some water."

So they started off, the seal so weak from thirst he could hardly walk. They went a long way before they came to three wells of water in the ground. It was all the seal could do to keep from diving right in as he lunged for the first well.

But the old crow said, "Wait! You can't drink at *that* well. Why, the idea of it!—a seal of your prestige and dignity. That well is the one slaves drink at. You can't drink there!"

So the seal, without a word, rushed on to the second well. But before he could immerse himself, the crow said, "Hold on! You can't drink at *that* well. That's not for a man of your position and prominence. Only the middle-class people—the ordinary villagers—drink there. You must quench your thirst at the well of the chiefs and rich men."

At that, the seal hurled himself without comment toward the last well. He plunged his head fully beneath the surface of the water and began gorging himself. He was completely dried out. Right away old *Chulyen* jumped at him and began pecking a hole in him to pull his guts out from behind. Just once the seal popped his head above the water.

"Ouch," he said. "What are you doing?"

"Why, you're so dirty," the crow said. "I'm trying to clean you up." And he went on pecking.

The seal was so thirsty he just dunked his head under the water again and kept drinking. Soon old *Chulyen* had pecked a hole right into the seal (for a seal's hide is tender) and pulled his guts out. The seal died then and the crow feasted on blubber for several days.

At the end of this time, when the meat had all been eaten, *Chulyen* changed back into a man. Returning to the water's edge, he launched his canoe and paddled on down the shoreline to a nearby village.

As he got closer *Chulyen* began crying so loud that even before he'd landed people from the village were running down to the beach to see what had happened. As they helped pull the canoe out of the water they asked him what was wrong. The poor crow explained to them through his tears how he and his partner —a seal—had been eating supper in camp and how the seal had gotten something caught in his throat and choked to death right before his eyes.

"And there was nothing I could do to help," he sniffled.

The villagers thought that was really a sad story, and they brought him up to tell it to the chief.

"Yes," *Chulyen* said, "it's true. I just lost my buddy. We were camped back down the shore a way, and we were eating when he choked to death."

At the very moment he was crying and telling this sad tale *Chulyen* belched, and up came a chunk of seal fat.

33

The villagers jumped to their feet.

"You're the one," they said. "You killed him and ate him."

They tried to grab old *Chulyen*, but he changed himself back into a crow and flew off. He made it safely out of the village, but lost his canoe in the bargain.

Soon after that the old crow made friends with a magpie and a water ouzel.

"We can kill bears together," he told them.

"How can we do that?" they asked him.

"Simple! One of us can just fly over and land near a bear. If you sit with your tail turned toward him, he'll think you don't see him and try to grab you. When he reaches out his arm, you can fly in quickly and cut him under his arm and kill him."

"I'll try it first," said *Chulyen*.

The first bear he tried it on was a big brownie fishing for salmon in a stream. The old crow flew up behind him and landed on a rock. The bear didn't see him at first, and *Chulyen* fidgeted for several minutes right behind him. But as soon as the bear turned and spotted him, *Chulyen* jumped backward and flew off.

"You're scared," they told him when he came back.

"No, I'm not," he said. "But you guys make too much noise."

The magpie decided to try it next on the same bear, and he surprised the others by lasting longer than *Chulyen* did. But when the bear started to reach out for him, he lost his nerve and flew off.

The water ouzel was sure he could do better than his partners, so after the bear had settled back down to fishing again, the tiny black bird flew over and landed right beside him, but facing the other way. Since the little bird's tail was toward him, the bear thought he had a meal for sure. But just as he reached out to grab it, the little ouzel swooped in and cut the bear under his arm and the bear died.

After that the water ouzel killed lots of bears for the three of them to eat. In fact, there was so much meat they had to build a house to store it in.

It wasn't long, however, before they noticed that the meat and fat seemed to be disappearing from the cache house during the nights. So one evening the little water ouzel hid inside the door of the house with a stick and waited to see who was stealing their food.

After dark he heard someone walking around outside. When the door slowly pushed open, the ouzel jumped out and began hitting the thief with his stick. But before he could capture him or tell who it was, the intruder ran off.

The next morning *Chulyen* showed up with scars all over him.

When asked about it, he said, "I hit myself with a stick."

But the magpie and the ouzel were suspicious now, and several nights later both of them waited inside the cache for the thief. When old *Chulyen* showed up they knew he was the one, but they waited until he was inside and starting to eat the meat before they jumped him.

"I wasn't stealing anything," he told them after they caught him red-handed. "You guys didn't tie the meat down very good and it was falling out. I was just fixing it up."

But they knew then, and they didn't want *Chulyen* around any more, so they chased him away.

"I never did like you guys anyhow," he yelled back at them as he flew off.

It was a crisp and beautiful spring afternoon, so *Chulyen* just flew around wondering what to do next. He sure felt like settling down in a village for a while, but everybody knew him too well. No one wanted an old crook like *Chulyen* around.

Late that same afternoon he flew over a village of geese. It was situated in a nice little bay, and the people seemed friendly enough, so he stopped in for the night. In fact old *Chulyen* liked the geese-people so well that he decided to spend the summer with them.

In time he fell in love with a goose-girl—the chief's daughter —and with the *cushka*'s permission they were married. (Proof of their marriage exists to this day. The Canadian brant and the Canada goose have a black head and neck, and several varieties have black feet. These are the descendants of *Chulyen* and his wife.)

But as fall rolled around, his brothers-in-law told him they would soon be heading south for the winter, and that he would have to stay behind and rejoin them in the spring. Old *Chulyen*, however, decided that he would go along.

"But it's such a long way," they insisted, "and we have to fly way out over the ocean. You'll never make it."

Chulyen knew better.

"If you fellers can make it, I can make it, too," he said. "Watch. I'll show you how well I can fly."

So he swooped into the air. He shot straight up until he was almost out of sight, then he tucked in his wings and dived. He rolled and flipped and twirled until all the geese were amazed.

After that, his brothers-in-law didn't feel they had the right to keep him from going along. They still didn't think he would make it, but what could they say?

So before long the stubborn old crow found himself stretched out in an arrowhead of geese, flying south for the winter. It took only a few days, however, for *Chulyen* to find out that what his brothers-in-law had told him was true after all.

They were flying high, way out over the Pacific Ocean, when *Chulyen* began to drop back out of the formation, unable to keep up. There was no place to land, yet he couldn't keep going. The geese didn't know what to do with him. In desperation, they began taking turns packing him. When one goose tired, another took his place, until finally the geese themselves began wearing out, and they saw that it just wasn't going to work.

So, after talking about it among themselves, they decided to drop him right where they were, or they would endanger their own chances of reaching their winter grounds. Even *Chulyen's* wife had to leave him and go on. If she stayed behind she'd freeze to death when it turned cold. At least this way he might make it to shore and back up the coast to home.

So, although they were sorry to do it, the geese wished him farewell, then flew right out from under him and beat their way south.

The crow pitched down, down, down. Old *Chulyen's* orneriness had really got him into a jam this time! But just before he hit, he went to work with that magical mind of his.

"I wish a rock would come up right under me."

And there was a rock. Right up out of the lapping waves a reef rose to meet old *Chulyen*, and he rested there for several days before turning homeward.

When he was ready to go, however, he had no idea which way to turn. But he took off on instinct, and flew for many hours toward the horizon.

Chulyen was just starting to get tired when he spotted a beluga floating lazily among the ocean swells. He dropped down to ask the long white whale for a ride.

"I'm lost," he said. "Will you take me to land?"

"Sure," said the beluga. "Crawl into the hole in my back and I'll dive. Then whenever you want to come up for air just holler."

So *Chulyen* burrowed into the whale's blowhole, and the beluga headed for shore. After a while the old crow hollered for him to surface, and he did. Climbing out onto the whale's back, *Chulyen* could already see the mountains in the distance.

Now when a beluga is just floating normally on the surface of the water, his eyes are still underneath, so he can't see above the water.

This is why he asked, "Can you see land yet?"

"No," said the crow. "All I can see is water."

So the beluga dived again and raced toward shore. A while later he returned to the surface, and once more old *Chulyen* crawled out on his back. They were almost to the shore.

"Can you see the land yet?" the beluga asked.

"I can just barely see the mountaintops way off in the distance," *Chulyen* lied.

"That's funny," said the whale. "I can feel the water getting shallower under me."

"Must be a reef," replied the crow. "Dive again and swim fast so we can reach the land soon. I'm anxious to get home."

So the beluga submerged again and swam his best. He went faster, and faster, and faster—until all of a sudden they ran right up onto the beach, way out of the water. And before the surprised beluga could squirm his way back down off the land, *Chulyen* jumped out on the beach and started throwing rocks into his blowhole. Soon it was so filled up the beluga couldn't breathe, and he suffocated to death.

The old crow started living inside the beluga's stomach that same night, feasting on the choicest of its insides.

The next morning as he was eating around inside the rib cage, the crow heard voices. Looking through a hole which he had chewed in the beluga's side, he saw two men approaching. *Chulyen* didn't want them to know who he was, so he flew straight up out of the blowhole like a shot until he was almost out of sight, then he turned and plunged into the woods way inland. There he changed himself into a handsome, well-dressed *cushkaveah*, and walked over to meet the two strangers.

When they saw him they wondered where he had come from. He told them he'd been just passing by when he saw them, and thought he would come down and say hello.

"We've found a dead beluga," they said. "But a strange thing happened. Something black came out of its stomach faster than the wind, and went straight up and out of sight."

"That's a bad sign," he said. "You'd better not eat any of that meat."

They agreed with him that it didn't look good. Then after they had talked some more, they invited him back with them to spend the night.

The two strangers lived in a village just down the beach around a couple of bends, so it wasn't long before old *Chulyen* was sitting with the chief in his *nichithl*. A sad story had already formed in the crow's mind.

"Yes, Chief," he said, "I am a *cushkaveah*, but my family once found a beluga lying on the beach when I wasn't around. They began eating on it, and every one of them died. I'm the only one left now."

Chulyen cried a little bit at this part, and the villagers felt sorry for him and invited him to stay with them, since he had no family. Of course the old crow was more than happy to stay there with them.

So he made the village his home for a while and married up with the chief's daughter. All the people liked him, since he was so handsome, and because he was married to her. They let him do just about anything he wanted.

Meanwhile, *Chulyen* was slipping out of the village every night to go down and feast on the dead beluga. But because everyone liked him so well, no one suspected anything. They even let him sleep in quite late in the mornings, so it was easy for him to stay out all night.

After a while people began noticing that the beluga was getting smaller, and they suspected that someone was feeding on it. But they never thought of old *Chulyen*.

"Naw," he said. "Nobody would eat that old stuff."

And because they liked him everybody believed what he said.

But finally the people started getting fed up with him because he slept so late all the time. So one morning several of the men came in very early to drag him out of bed to go to work. It was then they noticed that something was smeared all over his upper lip. When they looked closer they found his moustache was caked with beluga grease! Right away they knew what he'd been doing and who he was.

"You're *Chulyen!*" they yelled.

He came straight awake then and turned into a crow, but before he could fly off they grabbed him. They beat old *Chulyen* to death right there, then, after they had killed him, threw what was left out back of the village on the slop pile with the garbage.

An old woman found him lying there and cut off his nose. She stuck it in her needle case and threw his body back with the trash. Then she left.

After she had gone some magpies started flying around. They were screaming and hollering and defecating all over everything —including old *Chulyen*. It made him so mad he finally came back to life. According to legend, *Chulyen* is the magpies' uncle, and he thought they should have a little more respect for him. And he told them so.

But they went on chattering. "What're you doing out here?" they asked.

"Sleeping," he said.

"No you're not," they said. "You're dead."

He told them they were crazy, then asked where his nose was. They told him the old woman had it.

"Go away now," he said, "and let me rest."

As soon as the magpies left, *Chulyen* changed himself into a man and ran down to the beach. He bent over and began drawing bunches of men in *vudees*. Then he spoke to them.

"When I give you guys the signal," he said, "you come paddling around the point."

Then *Chulyen* flashed the signal and ran back up through the village holding his hand over his face (because he had no nose), and yelling that enemy boats were coming.

40

"Everybody run," he shouted.

Someone asked him why he was holding his hand over his face, and he was just going to tell them he had a toothache, when the *vudees* charged around the point. Everyone panicked.

"Run!" *Chulyen* cried. "Don't take anything with you. It'll just hold you back. Leave everything—especially your sewing boxes."

In three minutes the village was completely deserted. But the people had left everything behind, so old *Chulyen* changed back into a crow and started looking around for the old lady's sewing box. Finally he found it, and when he threw it open there was his nose.

Then he heard voices again. The people were coming back. So *Chulyen* scooped up his nose and stuck it back on his face and flew away. But he put it on in such a hurry that it was crooked, and all his descendants even today have that same crooked nose.

Chulyen was really angry.

"What can I do," he thought, "to get even?"

Then an idea came to his mind, and he went to work and built a footbridge across a canyon between two cliffs. When it was finished he went flying off over the whole countryside.

Whenever he would see an animal of any kind, he would shout, "Hey! I built a magic bridge. Come and see it!" Then he would lead them back toward the cliffs.

Finally, when he had drawn a huge crowd of bears, moose, wolves, beaver, wolverines, caribou, lynx, otter, mink, muskrats, and many other kinds of animals, he landed in front of them and started talking.

"This is a magic bridge," he said. "It can make you turn into a man. All you have to do is walk across it. When you step onto the other side you'll be a man. Watch!"

So old *Chulyen* waddled down onto the bridge and crossed over to the other side. As soon as he stepped onto the opposite cliff, he turned into a man.

The other animals were really impressed. They all wanted to try it out and started rushing for the bridge.

"Not yet," said old *Chulyen*. "My village is on the other side over that hill and I invite you all to a party. So everyone go home and get your families and bring them too, and we'll all go across together."

Everyone cheered for the crow and they raced each other home after their families. *Chulyen* just smiled.

Soon they were all back, leading hundreds of relatives, and *Chulyen* said:

"Okay. Let's go!" And he led the way down onto the bridge and across the canyon with the rest following.

It was a long footbridge. *Chulyen* had barely passed the middle when the last animal stepped onto it.

When the last one was well out over the canyon, the old crow turned and said:

"I told you this bridge was magical and that it could turn you into a man, but here's something I didn't tell you. Watch!" And he leaped into the air and began flying around.

"See!" he said. "This bridge also gives everyone who walks on it the ability to fly."

Once again the animals were really impressed.

"How do we do it?" they all cried.

"Just start jumping into the air," he said, "and pretty soon you'll start flying."

So the hundreds of animals began jumping up and down, up and down, until one end of the footbridge broke loose and they all fell screaming to their deaths.

Old *Chulyen* just flew around for awhile, waiting for the groaning to stop. Then, when it was quieter, he swooped down and began eating eyes.

After that, though, he had to leave the country because everyone who was left knew about him.

As the old crow flew on up the coastline, his conscience started to bother him, and he began to feel sorry about all the tricks he had pulled. He knew that it wasn't right, so he made a vow.

"The next chance I get," he told himself, "I'm going to try to help somebody instead of always hurting people."

Then *Chulyen* flew on until dark, and spent the night just outside a strange village. It was wintertime now, and it snowed a little and turned cold.

When he woke up the next morning the air was chilly and it was still dark out. *Chulyen* knew that night should be over because he'd had a good sleep, but there was no light at all—not even the moon. So he thought he'd go over to the village and see if anyone knew what the trouble was.

The people were up already when he got there, and everyone was huddled up talking in little bunches.

"What's the matter?" asked the crow. "Why is everyone so excited?"

"The *cushka* [rich man] has stolen the sun and the moon," said the people, "and he won't give them back. Now we don't have any light."

"Don't worry," said *Chulyen*. "I'll get them back for you."

So the cunning old crow put his mind to work, trying to figure out a way to get back the sun and moon for the people.

Now the rich man had a daughter who came down to the beach every morning to pack water. So the next day when she came down carrying a bucket old *Chulyen* was waiting for her, and when she scooped up a dipperful of water for herself, he dropped a small crow feather in it. She lifted up the dipper and gulped down the water in huge swallows—and along with it the crow's feather. Then she packed a bucketful back up to the house and went her way.

Soon after that the rich man's daughter discovered she was pregnant. People in those days didn't understand things as well

43

as we do today, so she wasn't really surprised. She just figured it was natural now since she was getting older that she was going to have children.

When her time came she had a healthy baby boy. He was a little guy, but he grew fast, and soon he was old enough to talk.

"*Chada* [Grandfather]," he said, "let me play with the moon."

Now the old man was really jealous of the sun and the moon, because he hadn't had them very long. But since it was his grandson, and he loved him so much, the old man gave his consent, and brought in the moon for the child to play with.

The little boy played and played until he got tired. Then he fell asleep and they took the moon from him.

When he woke up he cried, "*Chada*! *Chada*! I want to play with the sun."

So they brought him the sun, and he played with it for hours.

In the weeks that followed the little boy would often call out to his grandfather, "Can I play with the moon?" or "Can I play with the sun?"

Then one morning he awoke and cried, "*Chada*! *Chada*! Let me play with the sun and the moon!"

So they brought him both of the great lights and left him to play by himself. As soon as he was sure they were gone, a strange thing happened. The little boy changed into a crow. For all the time it had been old *Chulyen* in disguise.

He climbed out of the window and flew back to the village carrying both the sun and moon with him.

The mean old rich man felt so bad about losing his grandson that he really changed his ways. From then on he was kind to all his neighbors and never tried to steal the sun and moon again.

And as for *Chulyen*, the people were so thankful when he returned their sun and moon to the skies that they accepted him as a member of their village, and he lived there happily for quite a while.

44

First Brown Bear Story

T̲HERE WAS A GREAT UPROAR̲ in the village the day the handsome
stranger came. He was thick and tall and good-looking, and all
the young girls were impressed.

Before long he chose one of them to be his wife. She was the
envy of all the other girls, and when he took her home to live with
him each one wished it were she that was going.

The stranger lived upriver only a few bends from the village,
so it didn't take them long to get home. When they arrived he
surprised his new wife by telling her that he was a brown bear-
man, and that he didn't want any of her relatives coming around.

"If they do, they might find out who I am and try to kill
me. Then I would have to hurt them."

He promised that he would never harm anyone from the village and that he would treat her well, but he also gave her a
warning.

"If you try to leave, I'll find you and kill you."

The young wife was afraid of her brown bear-husband, but he
treated her all right, and although he always changed into a bear

45

when he went out hunting, he never failed to change back into a man before he came around the house.

As the years passed there were times when she almost grew used to living with a brown bear-man. But by the time their third child was born she had more reason to be afraid than ever. As the young ones were growing up they were fighting and wrestling all the time, and she realized that since they were her husband's children they were just like him.

One day the young wife's grandmother made a surprise visit. Nobody had told the old woman she wasn't supposed to come around. So when it was time for her to go, her granddaughter took a small piece of dead brush and cleaned out the inside of it. Then, after making her grandmother small, she stuffed the old woman into it and floated her down the river to the village. That way she wouldn't leave any scent or tracks.

When her brown bear-husband came home, he said, "I smell something strange. Somebody has been here."

"Oh," she said, "it's just the bodies you bring home that you smell."

He often brought home dead people and ate them, even though he always changed into a man himself before he entered the house. But he also brought squirrels and other meat for his wife because she wouldn't eat people. In fact, she really got angry at him for doing it.

She watched him sometimes as he played with his sons, and she could see that he was getting old. The sons were four or five years old themselves now and could whip him. She thought a lot of them and often told them never to go around the village. She didn't want them to kill—or be killed by—her relatives.

One day she finally confessed to her sons that she wanted to go back and visit her folks, but that their father wouldn't let her, and she was afraid of him. However, they had already read her mind.

"We know," they said. "We talk about it a lot. We're going to

46

do something about it, because he's too mean to you."

This only made her afraid for them, however, and she was sorry she'd told them. She was afraid their father would really hurt them.

But she couldn't stop them now, and from then on they were gone quite a bit of the time. Way off in the woods they were making a huge scaffold and piling rocks on top of it. They fixed it up with a spring-type lever so that when their father would walk underneath he would trip it and the rocks would fall on him.

After several days it was all ready. They tied a line to the stick that was holding it up and scattered leaves around the scaffold in the bushes. Even though they were old enough now and could probably whip him, they were afraid of their father.

Toward evening he came down along the trail as they had arranged. He was a huge old brown bear now. When he passed under the scaffold he tripped the lever. The sons had one last scare when he jumped as the rocks crushed down on top of him, but he was killed immediately.

They went back and told their mother.

"We killed Dad."

Then she told them how sorry she was that she'd told them, but they said, "Don't be. We read your mind anyway."

They said they were sorry it had to turn out that way, but they couldn't help it. They had to kill him.

So she took the sons and moved back to her old village. She told her people the whole story and about the boys' being brown bears. But she said they wouldn't hurt anyone as long as no one called them names or made fun of them.

Things went well for a long time. The boys fished in the ponds up behind the village as brown bears, and lived in the village as young men.

Then one day someone started teasing them and calling them brown bears. When he wouldn't leave them alone, they tore him in two.

Their mother was very sad, but she'd been afraid it wouldn't work out. She told her sons they'd better leave the village, and they did.

She often left the village herself after that to visit her sons, and the villagers made a pact with them. They wouldn't hunt down brown bears as long as they didn't come near the village or try to hurt anyone.

So the sons kept to their own grounds and lived in peace.

Second Brown Bear Story

ONCE UPON A TIME there was a great hunter living in the Old Village. Of all the men he was the most fearless, and whenever game was spotted up on the mountain—especially bear—he was always the first one to reach it. He had two good wives who were sisters.

One fall he began hunting more and more away from the village. He would be gone for weeks, and even months at a time. Then he was gone for the better part of a year.

When he finally returned to the village for the last time, he said that he was sick and was going to die. He told his wives not to bury his body or throw dirt over it, but to dig a hole for him and his weapons, and cover it over with his *bidarka* and sticks and grass. Then they were never again to come back to his grave. They were to leave him completely alone, and not come around disturbing his sleep.

Then one morning they found him as dead, and his wives started fixing up his grave.

After they had covered him over like he'd said, the sisters sat crying in the *gazhee*. Suddenly a white-headed chickadee flew down through the hole in the roof.

"Why are you crying?" he asked.

They told him how their husband had died.

"He isn't dead," said the chickadee, and promised to tell them more if they would knit him a cap, since it was getting colder outside. So they said okay, and while the first sister started knitting, the chickadee told his story.

"Your husband was visiting a girl in another village," the little bird began. "Then he started spending more and more time with her [which explained his absences from home] until he finally decided to marry her and go to live in that other village. He merely pretended to be dead," the chickadee said, "and is gone away even now to live with that other girl."

By this time the little black cap was finished, and the sisters placed it on the chickadee's head (this is the origin of the black-capped chickadee), and ran out to their husband's grave. Sure enough, when they rolled aside the *bidarka*, the grave was empty. The sisters were really angry.

They ran out of the village and turned into their *jonchas* (brown bears), and set off over the mountains. Hours later they came out on a ridge above a strange village. They were in plain sight of the distant houses—two big brown bears. Before long they were spotted and a group of hunters started up the mountain. Way out in front of the party a lone spearman approached them—the greatest hunter in this village, as he had been in the other.

As he drew back his arm to throw his spear, one of the wives pulled the mask up off her face to let their husband see who it was. Then she told him they were going to kill him. He begged and tried to make up to her, but she dropped the mask down over her face again and changed completely back into a bear. Then the two of them mauled him to death.

50

When the rest of the hunters got there, they were killed, too. And even then the bears did not stop. They ran down into the village and killed every single person there, including their husband's new wife.

Because they had done this, the wives could never turn back into people again, but had to remain bears until they died.

Afterward, the two bears began bickering and fighting with each other until they finally decided to split up. The meaner one moved south to Kodiak. The other one traveled north up into the interior. Even today the bears around Kodiak Island are meaner than their relatives up north, as proof of this story.

The Sea Gull Story

BACK BEFORE THE WHITE MEN CAME into the country, a young
Indian was snaring sea gulls on a large river in the falltime. As
the salmon spawned and died, and their bodies washed up on the
riverbanks, gulls and crows would hang around to eat them, especially around the mouths of the rivers where the fish were
thickest.

This young trapper had been having bad luck all fall. No matter how hard he tried he just couldn't seem to hold the gulls.
They kept making off with his snares and ruining his best sets.
So he started tying down the snares to heavier brushes and
deadfalls.

"That'll fix them," he thought. "Just let them try to fly away
with those things hanging around their necks!"

But he still kept losing snares, so he was forced to check
his sets more often.

Early one cold and foggy morning while he was going over his
line, he caught a freshly snared sea gull trying to fly away with

52

one of his sets. Since it was attached to a heavy stick, however, the gull couldn't carry it up into the air. By beating his wings as fast as he could, he was just able to drag it flopping along behind him on the ground.

"Hey, you! Stop!" cried the boy. "Come back here with my snare!"

But his yelling just scared the gull and it tried all the harder to escape. The bird flew along just above the ground, with the heavy length of wood dangling along behind. It was having a hard time, but going pretty fast.

The young Indian ran after it, yelling and trying to grab hold of the snare or the deadfall, but he couldn't quite catch up. The gull kept just ahead of him, flying for all it was worth.

The chase went on and on. The fog was so thick that several times the boy almost lost sight of the tricky gull. But then sometimes, too, it looked like he would catch it, he came so close. But he never got quite close enough.

All through the day the chase went on and the fog never lifted once. Pretty soon the boy realized that he was completely lost. He had no idea where he was. But since he'd come this far, he made up his mind to catch that gull. And the bird seemed to be weakening. He was sure it couldn't hold out much longer.

But he could see even through the fog that night was coming on, and if he didn't catch it soon it would be so dark he'd have to give up.

Just then the boy spotted lights up ahead. The bird seemed to be heading for them.

As he got closer, he could see that the lights were coming from the windows of a huge house, and the gull had disappeared. Figuring that the bird had gone inside, the young Indian pounded on the door with his fists. The door opened, and he rushed inside. The boy looked around and almost fainted from what he saw.

He had run into a huge room like his village *gazhee,* and

53

people like himself were lying all around on skins and blankets in pretty tough shape. Some had lost an arm or a leg. Others had scars and bruises, or strange-looking bindings fastened around their necks and waists. One man had passed out on the floor just inside the door. There was a long snare around his neck fastened to a large deadfall that lay beside him.

Then the young Indian realized that he had stumbled right into the home of the sea-gull people. He'd often heard the old-timers in his village say that birds and smaller animals were people just like themselves, and lived in their own homes and had their own families, but he'd never believed it. He'd even been bawled out by the old people for snaring gulls, but he'd just thought they were superstitious.

Now he realized the awful things he'd done, and he was really ashamed of himself.

But he knew that crying about it wouldn't help any, so he set right to work to fix up the damage he'd done.

First he took off all the snares from those who still wore them. Then he fixed up medicines from roots and plants to cleanse and heal those who were hurt.

The young Indian worked right on through the night. Those of the sea gull-people who were well enough helped him. Finally, along toward morning when he'd done all that was possible for the time being, he collapsed and they carried him to bed.

He slept long and hard, but when he woke up he went right back to work. Several days passed, and he never once left the house, but pushed himself hour after hour, doing all he could to help out. Because of his hard work and dedication he earned the respect of all the sea gull-people. They not only forgave him for what he'd done, but they liked him so well they invited him to stay there and live with them. The young Indian said he would do that, since he liked all the people so well, and they lived in such a beautiful country.

But the sea gull-people warned him about a small house down in the woods just below their own.

"If you stay here," they said, "whatever you do, don't go near that house."

When he asked them why, they said they couldn't tell him, but whatever happened he should never go near that house! So he promised them he wouldn't.

All went well at the big house for some time. More and more of the injured gull-people were up and around by the hour. They recovered quickly under the young Indian's care and they liked him better than ever.

Then one day as he was walking around at the edge of the woods in search of roots and plants to make medicines, he stumbled onto a *nichithl*—the little house about which the gull-people had warned him. Remembering what they'd said, and his promise, he was about to pass on by when he heard somebody whisper, "Sh-h-h-h. Sh-h-h-h."

It was a woman's voice, but he couldn't see where it was coming from. Then he spotted her over by the *nichithl* door. She was young and pretty, and seemed to be calling him over to the house. At first he thought he'd better not go, but then he got to wondering why everyone was afraid of such a pretty young girl. He figured he could take care of himself, and was curious, so he started walking over to her.

When he got right up close, she surprised him by grabbing him and yanking him right in through the door. She did it so fast she almost knocked him down. But she didn't seem anxious to hurt him, so he didn't try to resist.

Inside, the place was bigger than it had looked, and there was one strange feature about the room. Right in the middle of the dirt floor was a deep hole. The girl dragged the young man over beside it, and when he looked down in, he saw a gigantic, horrible-looking fat woman. She had skins and blankets and some other things right down in there with her. He figured she must have weighed about six hundred pounds.

"Mother," the girl said, "I brought a man."

The ugly woman said nice things to the young Indian then, but it still didn't make him trust her.

The girl invited him to sit down and have something to eat, so he did. His walk through the woods had made him hungry.

She went to the other end of the room and brought back a covered dish, which she offered to him. He took off the cover and started to reach into the dish, but when he saw that it was filled with human fingers he changed his mind. Now he realized that they were cannibals, and he thought he'd better play along carefully.

"No, thanks," he said. "I couldn't eat that stuff."

She shrugged and returned the dish. When she came back she told him that she wanted to marry him. He thought he'd better not argue with her, so he went along with her ideas.

They sat and talked for a long time, and soon it was bedtime. As they turned in, the young Indian noticed that it was really dark in the *nichithl*.

After a while he could tell by the girl's snoring that she was asleep. He breathed heavily and pretended that he was sleeping himself. Then he heard the fat old woman crawling up out of her hole and sneaking across the floor. When she got up next to the bed he could feel the heat of her breath on his cheek. She started feeling around to see which side of the bed he was sleeping on. She was soon satisfied and crawled back to her den.

The young Indian was really breathing heavily now, and he was cold with sweat. He knew that the old lady was up to no good. So as soon as she was back down in her hole he switched places with the girl without waking her up.

It wasn't long before he heard the sound of the old woman coming up out of her pit again and crawling across the dirt floor toward the bed. In her hand was a huge butcher knife.

The young Kenai made his voice sound like the girl's and whispered, "He's sound asleep now."

"O.K.," said the woman. "Where's his neck?"

He took her huge hand with his own and placed it on her daughter's neck. "Right there," he whispered.

At that she raised the knife high above her head, and plunged it into her daughter's neck, completely severing the head from the body.

The fat old woman then licked off the knife, but as she did, she became angry and cried, "*Yah dak' sheoo' cha ka dathl tin' a een l nish shid' ee*?" (How come this tastes so much like my daughter's blood?)

The young Indian thought fast.

"Our blood tastes alike," he said, still imitating the girl's voice, "because we're married."

The ugly old woman seemed satisfied with this and crawled back to her hole, looking forward to a feast in the morning.

Not until he heard her snoring heavily did the young man move. Then he quietly sneaked out the door and ran as fast as he could up to the sea gull-people's house.

They had been worried about him, for they'd guessed what had happened. After he told them what he had done, they were really afraid. For they knew that as soon as the six-hundred-pound woman found out what had happened, she would come after all of them.

But the young Kenai had a plan. He told the people to gather up two huge sacks full of rocks and help him set them up over the top of the door on the inside. They went right to work, and soon the job was done. Then they waited.

In the morning they heard a shriek. The woman had discovered her daughter's headless body. Then they heard her coming. She was crying, screaming, and singing all at the same time, telling how she had killed her daughter by mistake instead of the young man.

She was crawling on her hands and knees and belly, since she was so fat she couldn't walk, and carrying the monstrous butcher knife in her hand. With it she was cutting down everything in her path. The old woman had long arms and was hacking out a wide trail—not just grass, but brush and trees and anything else that got in her way.

Then she was in the doorway, screaming, "Where is he?"

And the sea gull-people yelled, "He's right above you!"

She twisted her head around to look up just as the young Indian cut the rope holding one sack of rocks, and five or six hundred pounds of them crashed down on her head. This stunned her for a minute, and the young man jumped down from his perch above the door. With one swing of an ax he lopped off her head.

But the woman wouldn't die. She fought blindly, wildly on, lashing out with her huge knife. Luckily, the young Indian had heard enough of the old village legends so that he knew what to do. He spit *k'entah* on the open wound and she died immediately.

It took several days for things to return to normal for the sea gull-people, and by that time their Kenai friend had decided to return to his own village. He told them that he liked staying there, but that he was homesick for his own people.

They understood, although they were sorry to see him go, and gave him instructions how to find his way home. Pointing back the direction from which he'd come, they said, "You must cross three mountain ranges. Then you'll see a house. There you will find a woman who will show you the way home."

Though it had taken him only one day to make the trip when he had been running after the snared gull, it took him three to find his way back. Finally he spotted the house he was looking for. He walked right in, and found an old woman sitting in a small chair. He asked her what direction he would have to go to find his way home.

"Do you know where you are?" she asked.

"No," he said, "I don't."

The woman reached down and pulled open a small trapdoor beside her chair and told him to look through it. When he did, he couldn't believe what he saw. He was way up in space! Far below he could see his family's fish village. He could even recognize his brothers and sisters. But he was clear up in the clouds! Somehow, when he'd been chasing the sea gull that foggy morning, the bird had led him through the secret passage from the earth below to its home in the sky. The young Indian was really scared. How would he ever get home?

The kind old woman, however, told him not to be afraid. She would get him down there. But he would have to help.

At her direction, the boy spent three days pulling up *kongalo-shee*, or Indian rope, in the woods. When she felt they had enough, she tied them all together into one long rope.

She made one end fast around his waist and said to him, "Now I'll lower you down. You will hit something, but don't open your eyes until you can reach out and feel grass on the ground."

So he slipped down through the hole and she began letting out the rope. He dropped lower and lower as she paid it out. Then he felt his body bump against something, and thought, "This must be the ground." So he opened his eyes.

The woman yanked him clear back up through the hole. "I told you that you would hit something," she said, "but it's not the ground. Don't open your eyes until you can feel grass."

So she let him down again and began paying out the rope. He felt his body hit something, but he kept his eyes closed. Then he bumped into something else. This time it was really solid. He thought, "I was fooled the first time, but I'm sure it's the ground now." So he opened his eyes, and immediately he was yanked back up into the sky.

The woman repeated her warning. "This is your last chance." She said, "If you don't keep your eyes closed until you feel grass this time, you'll never reach your home again."

So for the third time he dropped through the hatch and started

59

on the long trip down. Soon, he felt his body hit something. But he didn't look. Then he bumped into something else. But still he wouldn't peek. And a third time his body banged into something. But his eyes stayed closed.

Then his clutching hands brushed grass and he opened his eyes. He was lying on the ground.

His family had just finished putting up fish for the winter, and they were really happy to see him.

They soon found that he was one changed young man. Never again would he snare sea gulls or hurt them in any way.

There have been some who have doubted this story—especially the part about the young Indian's walking out into space. But the Giant of Lake Iliamna once did this very same thing when he was looking for his lost sister. If you don't believe it, on any clear night you can trace his footsteps in the stars across the sky in a long straight line.

Also, every spider that has spun a thread to drop down through space has done this in imitation of the young Kenai coming down on the *kongaloshee* from the sea gull's home in the sky. It especially makes you wonder when you run across a spider dropping from the sky at some distance from any trees if he, too, is not coming down from the same place.

First Eagle Story

THE TWO BROTHERS were young and handsome. They were the desire of all the girls in the village and could have had their pick of any of them. But they were young and didn't care much about girls.

Often the two of them would slip out of the village and run off deep into the woods. Far from home, they had cached two eagle skins in a tree. Draping these over their bodies, they would begin to shake furiously. (There is an Indian word for what they did—*co doz zle schish*, or "he shakes himself.") Then the two brothers would turn into their *jonchas*—a pair of eagles. They would rise into the air and glide for hours above the woods or out over the sea, hunting. They were proud of their young strength and beauty.

As the months passed, an older woman in the village who had not yet married was attracted to the boys and wanted them. First she tried to get one, and then the other. But they wouldn't have her. She wasn't an ugly woman—in fact, she was very good-

61

looking—and was hurt and insulted when the boys kept on ignoring her. She would get even, she promised herself.

So one afternoon when the boys slipped off into the woods, she followed them. And she was there watching when they turned into their *jonchas*.

As she watched them fly away a plan formed in her mind. She waited until they were almost out of sight, then switched to her own *joncha*, a sparrow hawk, and followed them.

The brothers flew farther and farther away from the village, until they were out over the waters of Cook Inlet. And still they didn't stop, but flew far out from land in search of beluga whales.

Then, when the eagles were miles out from shore, the hawk attacked. She charged right into them, slashing first one, then the other, knocking their feathers off and cutting them with her beak. The eagles tried to fight, but they were too young and not nearly as fast as the hawk, and they didn't have a chance. They kept trying to get back to shore, but as soon as they turned their backs on her, the hawk would slash them from behind. They grew weaker and weaker, and the hawk knew she was winning.

Far away, back at the village, the boys' father began to feel uneasy. He couldn't lose the feeling. Finally, when he could stand it no longer, he ran out of the village and turned into his *joncha*. Then, as a huge eagle, he climbed into the air and circled higher and higher, while the feeling in his heart grew stronger.

Then, suddenly, unexplainably, he knew his boys were in trouble, and that he must go to them.

Out over the ocean the battle was almost over. The young eagles had lost too many feathers, and were barely keeping themselves above the water. The hawk was taunting and slicing at them. A few minutes more and it would be all over.

Suddenly the hawk was smashed from behind and went reeling off into space. She turned to see a third eagle, larger and fiercer than the other two. It was the last look she ever got. The older, more experienced bird ripped her wide open, and she plunged into the inlet dead.

Then, with his wounded sons clutched to his back, the father winged his way back to the village and home.

Second Eagle Story

EARLY ONE MORNING a villager was out hunting when he spotted an eagle's nest near the top of a high cliff.

"I bet there are eggs in that nest," he thought. "I'd sure like some eagle eggs!"

So he went around the side of the mountain and climbed to the top of the cliff. When he looked over the edge and down into the nest he saw that he'd guessed right. There were several large eggs in it.

"I guess I'll just lower myself down to the nest and steal those eggs while the eagles are away," he thought.

So the young Indian pulled out some rawhide he had along, and tied it around a rock at the top of the cliff. Then he began lowering himself down to the eggs. When he was just about half-way, however, the rawhide frayed and broke, and he fell straight into the nest.

Right away he knew that there was no way up out of the nest, and that he would still be there when the eagles returned.

64

As the day passed, he became cold and miserable trying to hide in the nest, and he was tired.

Then the male eagle came home disguised as a man.

"You look scared," he told the villager.

"I was trying to get some feathers for my bow," the young man answered.

"Come inside," the eagle said, and the nest turned into a house. The intruder felt a little better, and went in to meet the wife.

They fed him. Then they gave him plenty of feathers for his bow. Afterward the male eagle said, "Put your head under my arm."

When the young man did as he said, the eagle flew him back to the top of the cliff and let him go home.

When he got back to his people, he told them the whole story. None of them ever hunted eagles anymore, or stole their eggs.

The Wolf Story

EARLY ONE SPRING a young man and his wife walked up a mountainside far from their village packing a small baby. They pitched camp near the top, and spent the next weeks making snares of eagle feathers for trapping mountain squirrels. After the trapping started, they were usually gone from their camp most of the day.

One evening they came back late after a hard day on the mountain. The young man was leading the way with his wife following behind, packing the baby. When they reached the tent he drew back the flap and held it for her as she stooped over and passed inside. When she straightened up in the dark interior, the young woman was completely taken by surprise. Lying there just in front of her was a huge gray wolf. Her husband was still outside, and she didn't know what to do. Then an idea struck her, so she stooped down and laid the baby right beside the wolf.

"Here's your little brother," she said to the wolf. "We just found him."

66

The wolf started licking the baby's face.

When the young man stepped inside, he saw what had happened and he spoke to the wolf. As he talked the wolf's ears went back, so they knew it understood what he was saying.

A strange companionship began to develop. From that time on the wolf stayed with the family and hunted with them high on the mountain. The couple treated him like a son, and the wolf accepted the child as his baby brother. Sometimes he would take it from the cradle and carry it out into the woods or off around the mountain for hours at a time. Whenever the father went hunting for caribou he took the wolf with him. When they'd spotted a herd the wolf would rush in to slaughter all they needed, so the family never went without meat.

As the boy grew older, the wolf taught him how to hunt. He learned fast, but the wolf was never satisfied and pushed him harder and harder. He made him run and work until the boy was faster and stronger than anyone else his age had ever been. He was so quick he could catch birds in the air.

After a while the boy's father began to grow jealous of the wolf. The boy was always running off some place with him, and his wife was forever saying what a good hunter the wolf was.

So one day when he was feeling mean, the boy's father took the wolf out with him to run down some caribou. It wasn't long before they came upon a herd and the man sent the wolf off after them. In a few minutes it had killed four, and the man followed along behind and started cleaning them.

It had always been his habit as he gutted the animals to wash off the liver and give it to the wolf. This time, however, he left the liver all bloody and simply threw it at the wolf, hitting him in the face.

"You're no wolf," said the man. "You're half dog. We don't have to wash everything for you all the time."

The wolf just sat there looking at him. It didn't eat the liver.

When the man had finished loading up his pack, he hoisted it to his shoulders and started off.

The wolf still sat there with blood on his face getting madder and madder. He watched until the man was far off in the distance. Then he leaped up and was after him like a shot. He caught up to the man and killed him there with the pack still on his back.

When the man didn't come home for supper that night, his wife suspected that something had happened to him.

Later that evening she went to the door and found the wolf lying there with blood all over his face.

"I guess he has killed my husband," she thought.

Kneeling beside the wolf, she began washing off his face while she talked to him.

"What happened to my husband?" she asked. "Did you kill him?"

Both of the wolf's ears twitched forward, so she knew that was what had happened.

After she had fed the wolf, he lay down near the doorway and fell asleep.

Later on, while the woman was nursing the boy, she started feeling bitter about what the wolf had done.

"I'll get even with him for killing my husband," she thought.

So while he slept, the woman took her own milk and rubbed it all over the wolf's paws. She knew that after a while that would make his feet so soft he wouldn't be able to walk. She didn't want to kill the wolf, but she wanted to make him sorry for what he'd done.

When she had finished, the woman began moving around the tent getting together her belongings. Soon the wolf woke up and she said:

"There's no use in my staying around here anymore. I'm going back home to my village. You won't be able to go along, of course."

The wolf sensed her bitterness now, and so he turned into a man and explained to her exactly what had happened. As he told his story, the wolf-man stood beside the boy holding on to him. The woman began to feel sorry for what she had done to his feet, but was afraid to tell him about it.

He said he realized that because he was a wolf he couldn't come into the village to live with them, but promised that he would still do what he could to watch out for the boy.

"Whenever you fellows are having a hard time in the village," he said, "and you don't have enough food, just listen for a wolf howling. Go to where the sound is, and you will find meat."

Then he left them.

A year passed, and the young boy and his mother didn't see the wolf again even once. The following winter a famine struck the village. The women set snares out all over the woods, but there weren't any rabbits. The men hunted clear back into the mountains, but the country was empty of game.

Then one night as the men returned empty-handed from a hunting trip, they heard a wolf howling not far from the village. They thought nothing of it but the young woman heard them mention it when they came in and she knew what it meant.

Early the next morning she rushed out to where the wolf had been heard and found him waiting.

"I've brought meat for you," he said.

Then he turned into a man and cleaned the game for her and built a scaffold to put it on until she could return for it with the others.

When she'd finished loading up her pack, the young woman said to the wolf, "The men from the village will be coming here after this meat. You'd better not be around or they'll kill you."

"I only came to make sure you have enough meat," he said. "I'll be gone before they come."

As he turned away the woman saw that he was limping and

69

she knew that his feet were getting softer. But she didn't know how to tell him what she'd done.

That afternoon when she got back to the village the woman told everyone where the meat was, and the men all hurried out to pack it in. There was plenty to last until the hunting got good again, and everyone was happy. Life was better in the village after that, and the winter months passed quickly.

But by spring there were other problems. Some of the people said they had seen a wolf in the village. Others said it had stolen from them. After much talking the men finally got together and said they would hunt it down and kill it.

When the young woman heard about it, she ran out to look for the wolf. She knew that she must find him before the hunters did. Finally, after hours of searching, she found him. He walked over to her and sat down. Then he lifted a covering like a hood from his face and turned into a man.

"Look at my feet," he said. "They're all raw."

He confessed to her that he had been stealing meat from the village. His feet were so sore that he couldn't run down any game for himself.

The young woman finally broke down and told him what she had done to his feet, but said she was really sorry and promised to help him. She took some pieces of skin out of her sewing kit and put them under his feet. When she had spit on them, they stayed on, and the wolf's feet were all right again.

So he put his hood on again and changed back into a wolf. Then he began running around so fast she couldn't even see him. He was so happy he forgave the young woman for what she had done. He even told her that if they ever needed meat in the village again, he would still be glad to get it for them.

The woman told him he'd better keep out of sight for a while though, because the men would be out hunting him. She also warned him not to take any more meat from the village.

"It might be poisoned," she said.

So they split up, and the woman went back home to her son.

The boy was getting older now, so she told him what had happened. After that he always went along whenever the wolf left food for them. And sometimes he would go out alone to meet the wolf and the two of them would go hunting together.

As the years passed, the time came when the boy was no longer a child but a man. He married, and built a cabin on the shore of the lake not far from his mother's village.

It was then the wolf decided to have a serious talk with him.

"I am your brother," the wolf said. "I've taught you a great deal and you have learned well. But now you must go on your own. You are a great warrior. I'm getting old now, and you could even outfight me. But one day all the animals will make war on you—because I have taught you and you have killed so many of them—and you cannot outfight them all. So you must prepare yourself for that day.

"The first thing you must do is make a home out on the island and cache food there. Next, be sure you have a skin boat ready at all times. Then, when all the animals attack, you can jump into the boat and row out to the island."

The young man hurried to carry out his friend's instructions. Having lived with the wolf all those years, he knew that whatever he said was true. Before long everything was ready.

Then one night, when he and his wife were asleep, the young man was wakened by strange noises coming from the woods. He woke her, and they hurried down to the beach and piled into the skin boat. They had barely pushed out from shore when the clearing around his cabin filled with raging animals.

Among the animals was a large gray wolf, and after the man and his wife were out of earshot, he turned and said:

"You see! I told you we couldn't catch him. He's too fast."

The rest of the animals didn't know the man was the wolf's brother.

Several nights later a skin boat moved soundlessly across the

71

water from the island and touched shore just below the cabin. A lone figure slipped out onto the beach, moved quietly up the shore to the house, and peered in through an open window.

All the animals were inside having a feast on some groundhog meat the man had left behind when he escaped. The king of the beasts sat at the head of the table. Fitting an arrow to his bow, the man stood up, drew back, and let it fly. The shot pierced the animal king to his heart, and he dropped over dead.

The cabin was in an uproar. All the other animals jumped up and were milling around, but by the time some of them scrambled outside to catch him, the man was already in his skin boat paddling back out to the island.

Once again the old wolf told them, "You see. I warned you we could never catch him."

A few nights later the young man returned in the boat with his wife. Again he sneaked quietly up to the cabin. But when he reached the porch someone was waiting for him there in the shadows. It was the old wolf. He'd been expecting him.

The wolf handed the young man a *dukh'oe*—a moose-bone club—and said:

"You may kill them all, or let some escape—whatever you want."

The man understood. He kicked open the door and rushed inside, swinging the club right and left. He didn't stop until he had killed every animal he could get his hands on, and the cabin was still with death. Only a few had escaped. Finally, when his anger and strength were gone, the man walked out onto the porch. The wolf was satisfied.

"The few that got away talked to me before they left," he told the man. "They said to tell you they forgive you, and that they are going to have a party in two years at the dead king's house. You and your wife are invited."

"What are they going to do?"

"It is a trick. They are going to try to kill you then."

But the wolf said that he would be back before the time came to talk with him about it.

"Meanwhile I'll watch out so that nothing happens to you or your family."

The months passed rapidly, summer and winter, and before it seemed possible the two years were up and the wolf returned.

"They are getting all ready now," he said, sitting down. "The party will be in about two days, so you must prepare yourself. First, go out and kill several brown bear and caribou so you can make some bone clubs. Then fill the clubs with oil and freeze them. This will make them very heavy. Make plenty of them— some for your wife too.

"The animals will be ready for you, but I'll do what I can to help. When you find them I will be there."

So the young man hurried to get everything ready. He made the oil clubs and fixed up his bow with plenty of arrows. His wife kept busy sewing skins together so they would be waterproof. She would fill the skins with oil and freeze them into clubs also.

When the weapons were finished, the man and his wife collected them and started walking to where the party was going to be.

Just before they got there, the young man stopped at the home of an old woman who lived in a foxhole right under the trail. He told his wife to wait outside the door for him.

Inside, the old woman was sitting down. She lived all by herself.

"Who are you?" she asked.

He told her his name. She said the animals were going to make war on a guy by that name.

"I'm the one," he said. "I killed your king."

The old woman started to scream, but he knocked her down with his oil club and smashed her throat before she could make any noise. She died.

The young man called to his wife as he began skinning the old woman out. Together they waited in the foxhole until nighttime. Then he put the old woman's skin over himself and picked up her cane and left with his wife for the party. His wife wouldn't need a disguise because the animals didn't know her.

Pretty soon they came to the place where the party was supposed to be. It was just like a little town—a village of animal people.

When the young man and his wife entered the dead king's house, the wolf, who was there ahead of them with his own wife, recognized his friend.

"That's your brother-in-law," he whispered to his wife. "Go invite them over."

So the young man and his wife went over and sat down with the wolf and his wife. Later in the evening the two brothers left the party together and had a talk outside.

"They'll all be starting home pretty soon now," said the young man. "They don't think I'm coming. So I'm going to wait right here by the door in the dark and kill them as they leave."

The wolf told him not to kill *all* the animals, but to leave a male and female, or at least a female, of each kind so they would not die out completely.

Then the wolf went back inside and began talking each of the party guests into leaving, one or two at a time, while the man stood outside the door, killing some and letting some go.

When the house was about half empty, those left inside suddenly started getting nervous, as if they knew. They all abruptly changed back into animals and ran off, streaming out the back door and windows.

The man and his wife went inside and walked all around, taking whatever they wanted.

"You're too smart for me," said the wolf.

"What do you mean?" asked the young man, turning to his friend.

"I thought they would get you. But now there won't be any more war again, ever.

"I must go now," the wolf said, "for I am getting old. But there is one thing you must always remember. Whenever any animal attacks or charges you, just think of me. I'll be right by your side. None of them will be able to catch you or hurt you in any way."

This pact between the wolf and the young Indian has held good through many generations of their descendants. Michael A. Ricteroff's grandfather, Old William Ricteroff, was trapping foxes out of Old Iliamna Village one winter when he accidentally caught a wolf.

Recalling the friendship between his ancestors and the wolf's, he approached the animal, speaking to it in low tones. He apologized to the wolf, explaining that he had not meant to trap it, but that it had been an accident. The wolf's ears lay back, showing that he understood.

So Old William stooped down and released the trapped paw. The wolf walked off a few steps, then stopped and looked back before loping away.

It was the best season's trapping Old William ever had. His traps were filled all winter with foxes and lynx.

The Black Bear Story

LATE ONE FALL two villagers went bear hunting on a mountain a few miles upriver from their home. They'd just worked their way above and along the timberline about a mile when they spotted three black bears—two old ones and a cub. The hunters sneaked up on them while the bears were playing in a rock slide. When they came within range, one of the hunters said to himself, "I'm going to marry that black bear."

So he turned and killed his partner. Then he shot the male bear.

He had a tough time making up with the female after that, but he disguised himself as a black bear, and by the first snowfall went into hibernation with her and the cub.

Sometimes she would wake up and look around and sniff.

"What's the matter?" he'd ask.

"I smell something strange."

"There're no men in here," he'd say.

The disguised villager stayed with the bears all that year and the next. But by the following spring he'd begun to tire of that life. He decided that he really didn't care for it, after all. So he left the bears and went back home.

Years later, two villagers were squirrel hunting on the same mountain. One was setting snares and really working hard, but the other one just sat around eating berries. They were supposed to be partners, so the first one said to the other one, "Why don't you work hard?"

"Oh, I don't know," said the second hunter as he filled his mouth with berries. "I just don't want to."

One day a few weeks later the hard-working partner found it necessary to go back down the mountain to the village, and leave the snares for the lazy one to watch.

It was some time before he was able to return, and when he did he had a surprise waiting for him. On his way up to the camp he passed several of their snares and traps, and they were all full. His partner hadn't checked them once since he'd left.

When he finally reached camp, he found his partner sitting around eating berries.

"Why didn't you run the traps?" he asked.

"Oh," said the partner, as he scooped in another armload of berries, "I just didn't want to."

The first hunter was still puzzled and a little bit angry when, several days later, he heard his berry-eating partner singing off in a field beside some trees. He had an idea. With the greatest care he sneaked up on him. When he got right up close, he suddenly jumped up and screamed.

The partner in the berry patch was so surprised and scared that he jumped up and turned into a black bear and ran away.

It was the same man who had killed his partner years before so he could marry a black bear. Now he was one.

He got what he wanted, but he didn't want what he got.

The Fox Story

ONCE THERE WAS A MAN who met two sisters. They came to his place and stayed with him. They were nice-looking women with long brown hair tied in knots behind their heads in the old style. He took them for his wives.

They were a strange family. Whenever things got tough and there was no food, the wives would say to him, "You stay here." Then they'd go out with tiny packs. When they came back, they'd throw them down, and so much food would fall out and pile up that there would be plenty.

After a while, they took him back to their house in the side of a hill. There were lots of people there, and they were forever short on food. But the two wives always went out and brought back plenty.

Finally one day he said, "You women always get the food. I'll get it this time."

So they told him how to get food, "Just go around people's

houses and gather up crumbs. It will add up. Only don't do anything wrong."

This puzzled him. Then when he went outside the house he found fox tracks all around. He began to suspect that they were fox-people.

He remembered how they'd warned him not to do anything wrong, and he wondered what they'd meant.

By this time he'd reached the fish ponds back in the woods. There were lots of fall fish and meat crumbs lying around. He ate and ate until he was full. Then he figured it was too much work to pack lots back. So he only took one old dried-up salmon with him.

On the way back he kept thinking about what they'd said about not doing anything wrong, and wondering what they'd meant. He couldn't figure out how his wives could bring in such huge piles of food.

"This little bit I brought wouldn't swell up like that," he thought to himself.

But he started feeling funny as he neared his home. He was getting heavier and heavier. When he got back to the house he couldn't get in the door. Two foxes came out.

He said, "Are my wives in there?"

They said, "Yes," and went to get them.

When his wives came out, they were really surprised.

"What did you do?" they asked.

"I just found some crumbs and ate them."

"See!" they said. "We told you not to do anything wrong. Those crumbs swell up. Just look at yourself."

His stomach was huge.

Then they did something to him and he returned to normal.

"I'm going to try again," he said.

So off he went, picking up meat crumbs, and fish crumbs, and bits of fat. Then he bundled them all up in a rag and tied it.

When he brought his package home and dumped it out, food piled up on the floor until there were great bundles of fish, and dried meat, and heaps of fat. His wives were really surprised.

A few weeks later he took them back to his village with him.

Before long someone found out about his wives. His people told him they were dirty old foxes. "Thieves," they said.

His wives heard about it, and they ran off.

The next morning someone came in and told him his wives were running away. He hurried outside, but he saw that they had changed into foxes and were already a long way off.

He chased after them, but lost them when they got out of sight. However, he knew where their den was, so he went there.

Two foxes met him at the door. But they turned into women, and he saw they were his wives.

Before he could say anything, they apologized for running off.

He apologized too, and said he hadn't known about them.

They asked him to come into the den, but the hole was too small and he said he didn't know how to get in there.

"Close your eyes," they said, "and put your sleeve over your face."

So he did, and when he leaned against the hill . . . WHAM! . . . he fell inside. He got up and found lots of people around him having a good time. He was a fox now, too, and stayed with them there the rest of his life.

The Mountain Squirrel Story

THERE USED TO BE a mountain squirrel-woman who had ten husbands. One day she got angry at them and walked off down the mountain. She walked a long way through other mountains and visited lots of people.

Then one morning she saw what looked like a big beaver house. She walked down to it, and a woman sitting by the door said, "Come in."

So the mountain squirrel-woman followed her. It was a big house inside with lots of rooms, and she met some other people who gave her berries to eat.

"Are you going to stay here, or move on?" they asked her.

"I'll stay here," she said.

They let her choose her own room, so the woman selected a good one and lay down.

"You sure picked out the wrong room," they told her. "The man who owns that bed never comes home."

They explained that it was their custom that whoever owned

the bed a stranger chose became the stranger's mate. However, she wouldn't be able to marry this man, they said (although they wouldn't say why). But he would feed her, even if he did act peculiar sometimes and come in at all hours.

Late that night, as the mountain squirrel-woman lay in bed, he finally came in. But he went right to sleep without saying anything at all.

He was a strange man. Whenever he and the other men came home with berries or meat, he would fill his wooden plate and go into the hallway leading to another room. Then the wall would open up, and when he had stepped through, it would close behind him. No one else ever went in there, and no one ever came out. Yet he would stay in there for hours.

He was a handsome man, but he never paid much attention to the new woman who had moved in with him. In fact, he scarcely seemed to notice she was there.

One night as he came out of the wall in the hallway, a plate came sailing right out past his head. Someone had thrown it.

"That's strange," thought the mountain squirrel-woman. "I wonder who's doing that."

Another evening as she sat by the fire, the first woman she'd met came by.

"Are you hungry?" this woman asked.

"Yes," said the mountain squirrel-woman. "Thank you."

As they began eating nuts together, she said to the woman, "You were right about that man."

"I told you."

"Do you know who's in that room in the hallway? He goes in there and stays all night."

"Sure, I know. It's the rich man's daughter. She lives in there, and all she ever does is sit in a swing. Your man goes in there to swing her. Whatever you do, don't try to marry him. Her father is so rich that she has beads for eyebrows."

"Beads?"

82

"Beads!"

"Can I go in there?"

"No."

This made the mountain squirrel-woman more curious than ever.

Then one day when she was walking through the hallway, she passed too close to the wall, and suddenly it opened up right beside her. Before she could move, a stick reached out and grabbed her by the hair and pulled her in. The last thing she could remember was the wall's closing behind her, and her being thrown into a swing, or cradle, right across the room from Beads Eyebrows. Then she became sleepy and passed out.

Much later, the mountain squirrel-woman came to in a room where she didn't recognize anything. All she could think of was that stick, and she hurt all over so much she could hardly breathe.

Gradually she realized that she was in a swing, being pushed by a man she didn't know. He acted strange, as if he were doped, and didn't know what he was doing.

The mountain squirrel-woman could look around, but she was unable to move or speak. She sat like that in the swing all day.

Toward evening Beads Eyebrows looked at the wall and pointed with her magic stick. It opened, and the strange young man walked in.

Beads Eyebrows said to him, "Go see your wife."

With her stick she threw him over beside the mountain squirrel-woman. The man saw how she'd been beat up, and that she couldn't move or speak, just look around.

"Well," said Beads Eyebrows. "How do you like it?"

The man looked at the stranger, then back at old Beads Eyebrows, and saw that the younger woman was prettier.

"You go swing your wife," he was ordered.

So he did, and the mountain squirrel-woman began to get better.

Beads Eyebrows pointed her magic stick into a corner and another swing came down. Then the wall opened into a hidden room, and she pulled a man in with her stick and threw him into that swing. A slave was forced to swing him.

"You swing your own wife," Beads Eyebrows said to the young man swinging the mountain squirrel-woman. "That man [she pointed to the one in the other swing] will be my husband."

With her magic stick Beads Eyebrows pulled her new husband from his swing into her own beside her. He had beads for eyebrows, too.

Then the man who was swinging the mountain squirrel-woman appeared to have a change of heart. He walked over to Beads Eyebrows to talk to her.

But when he got close, he tricked her and snatched the magic stick from her hand. First he opened the wall and let the mountain squirrel-woman out of the room. Then he closed it again and threw Beads Eyebrows out of her swing.

"It's all right now," he said. "He's your husband. Now you swing him."

So with the power of the magic stick he made Beads Eyebrows swing her new husband, and he left the room to go to his new wife, taking the stick along.

As he went out, the young man closed the door behind him, and it was never opened again.

The Cat Story
(The Magic Ring)

THERE WAS ONCE an old married couple who were very poor and had no children.

One night while the man was on his way to a distant village, a brown bear jumped him. Two hunters came by and saw what was happening, and killed the bear right away; but the old-timer was pretty bad off, so they packed him back to their home and took care of him until he was better.

A few weeks later the old man was back on his feet, so he left there to go back to his wife. Toward evening he was walking along the beach when he heard someone scream and saw something out in the salt water. A young girl was drowning, so he jumped in the water and swam out to save her.

When he finally got her back on the beach, she told him, "My father is a rich man. He'll give you any reward you name. When he asks what you want, tell him you'd like his ring."

"Why?" the old man asked. "I don't know anything about his ring."

"It's a gold ring," she said, "and it's magic."

"What do you do with it?"

"If you want a house or anything, just take it out of its handkerchief and spin it. Two short little guys will come in, dressed just the same, like twins. Tell them whatever you want, and they'll do it or get it for you. Then, whenever you want them to leave, just spin the ring the other way and they'll disappear."

So the old man followed the girl home.

"How much do I owe you for saving my daughter?" her father asked. "I'll pay you anything you say."

"Your magic ring," said the old man.

"How did you find out about that?"

"I just heard about it."

"Well, I sure hate to part with it," said the girl's father. "But I'll think it over."

The girl had overheard them talking and went up to her father.

"If it weren't for the old man," she said, "I wouldn't be here now."

"You're right," her father said. "O.K., I'll do it."

So he called in the old man and gave him the ring wrapped in a large handkerchief. He thanked him again for saving his daughter's life and said, "Here, let me show you how it works."

He took the ring out of the handkerchief, set it on the table, and gave it a spin. Right away a pair of short twins came into the room. The girl's father spoke to them, "This guy is going to be your new master, you two. Do whatever he tells you."

They nodded, and he spun the ring backwards, causing them to disappear.

Before the old man left, the girl's father shook his hand, thanked him again, and gave him some money in addition to the ring. He also reminded the old-timer that the ring could be used his whole lifetime, and warned him not to lose it.

Then they parted, and the old man went home to show the ring to his wife and all their friends.

The first thing he did was have the twins build him a big house. Then he hired them out to others and began to grow very rich.

The old man's wife, however, was getting jealous over the ring, because he would never let her have it. So, one night after he went to sleep, she stole the magic ring out of his pocket.

When he woke up the next morning, the old man started out for a nearby village. He didn't tell his wife the reason for his hurry, but he planned on winning more money with the gold ring by gambling with some guys who didn't know he had it.

As soon as she was sure he was gone, the wife pulled out the magic ring and gave it a spin. When the twin men appeared, she told them she wanted a house built just for her on the other side of the river and downstream a way. Also, she wanted them to put a bridge across the river at the same spot, so she could cross forth and back easily.

When she'd finished with her orders, the twins went off, and before nightfall the house and bridge were both complete. So she left her husband's home and went to live by herself.

Meantime, the old man had discovered his ring was missing, and guessed his wife had taken it. Luckily, however, he had a faithful old cat along with him, who followed him everywhere he went. It was a really smart cat, so the old man told it to go back home and find the magic ring, then bring it back to him there at the village.

The cat ran all the way back to their home, but when he got there, he couldn't find the ring or the old-timer's wife. So he looked around until he found her tracks, and followed her—down the river, across the bridge, and over to her new house. By then it was late at night and dark.

Just then the cat spotted a little mouse running across the

porch. He pounced and caught the little guy but didn't kill him.

Pretty soon a big mouse came out and said, "That's my kid you've got there. Let him go."

"If you go inside," the cat said, "and get that handkerchief with the ring in it and bring it out here, I'll trade you the kid for it."

The mouse said it was a deal and ran inside to fetch the ring. Soon he returned, dragging the handkerchief and ring behind. The cat let the baby mouse go, then he picked up the handkerchief and ring and ran back down to the bridge.

As he was crossing, however, the ring slipped out of the handkerchief and dropped down through the bridge into the water. The cat ran down to the beach and paced back and forth. Then he sat down and started crying.

But as he sat there a trout fingerling swam a little too close and the cat jumped and caught it. Pretty soon, a big trout swam up. "Let him go," said the fish. "That's my baby."

"I lost a gold ring in the water," the cat said. "Get it for me, and I'll trade you."

The trout disappeared, but in a minute was back with the ring, and the cat gladly traded the fingerling for it. Then he ran off to bring it to his master.

Meantime, the old man had been taking bets on his magic gold ring. No one believed his story. But when the cat returned, he pulled it out of the handkerchief and gave it a spin. The twins appeared and did everything he told them. So he collected on all his bets.

Later, when he found out about his wife's new house, he had the twins tear it down. They did it at night while she was sleeping, so that when she woke up she was surprised to find she had no house.

But she had one more surprise coming. When she tried to move back in with her husband, he turned her away and wouldn't have anything more to do with her.

The Wolverine Story

ONE DAY IN EARLY WINTER all the people from the village were out in the timber cutting wood together. They were stocking up for the colder days ahead of them. Even the *cushka*—the rich man, or chief—was right out there chopping with the rest, when he could have had his *noglthna*, or slaves, work in his place.

The sound of axes filled the woods and there was a good feeling in the air. Then someone cried out, "A stranger is coming!"

Everyone stopped and looked. When they saw him, they all threw down their axes and went over to meet the visitor, for they didn't often have company in the village in those days.

He was a short, stocky man—almost fat, even. He told the people he had come a long way.

But he didn't tell them that he was an *edashla*, or wolverine, and that he was only disguised as a man.

Now the *cushka* had three good-looking daughters, and the visitor said this was why he had come. He wanted to marry the oldest one.

But he didn't tell the *cushka* that the reason he wanted to marry her and take her home was because he wished to eat her.

So the chief invited the visitor to his *nichithl* for tea. He wanted to introduce him to his daughters and get to know him better.

After they'd visited a few hours, the chief decided the stranger would be a good provider, and would treat his daughter kindly, so he said they could get married.

There wasn't such a thing as a formal wedding ceremony in those days. The visitor just took the girl home the next morning to live with him.

He walked so fast the girl could hardly keep up with him. Yet even at that rate it took them all day to reach his home. By the time they finally got there she was so exhausted from the trip that she didn't even notice her new husband had lied to her father—he didn't live in a village as he'd said, but in an isolated *nichithl*. There wasn't another thing in sight.

When she entered his little pole house all the girl wanted to do was fall down and go to sleep. But he denied her even that. As soon as he closed the door behind them, he grabbed her, threw her down, and tied her up. She watched as he uncovered a hole hidden under the fireplace in the center of the room. Then he dragged her over and rolled her into it. He told her that he was an *edashla* and that he was going to starve her to death and eat her. Then he covered the hole over again with the girl down in it and headed back toward the village.

The next morning he stood talking to the *cushka*.

"You have a fine daughter," he told the chief. "She's a good wife and I'm pleased with her. But she says she's lonely, and wishes one of her sisters could come stay with us to keep her company."

The request sounded reasonable, so the chief gave his permission.

That same day *Edashla* left the village with the *cushka's* second daughter. She, too, found it difficult to keep up with him, and was completely worn out by the time they reached his *nichithl*.

As soon as she stepped inside, *Edashla* knocked the girl down and tied her up. Then he uncovered the hole under the fireplace and threw her in with her sister. He whistled to himself as he covered them back up.

It was just turning light the next morning when he stood telling the *cushka* that the girls desired the company of their younger sister. Still unsuspecting, the chief again said all right, and his last daughter got ready for the trip.

Unlike her father, however, the youngest daughter suspected something was wrong. She didn't trust old *Edashla*.

As usual, the old wolverine set off walking very fast, hoping to wear the girl out right away, but this time it wasn't so easy. The third daughter was younger and more athletic than the others and kept up with him easily. Two or three times he tried going faster, only to find that the girl adjusted to it more easily than he did.

Long before they reached his *nichithl*, old *Edashla* was staggering. He could see that, as tired as he was, he wouldn't be able to overpower this girl as easily as he had the others, so he changed his plans a little. He decided to keep her around for a couple of days until he was more rested. As healthy as she was, he figured he could get a lot of work out of her that way before he threw her in with the others.

When they reached his house, *Edashla* burst straight in and collapsed on some skins in the corner. The girl followed him inside, but kept standing. She wasn't even breathing hard.

"Where are my sisters?" she asked.

"Oh," he panted, "they're probably out hunting or cutting wood. They should be back soon."

She didn't show it, but this made the girl more suspicious than ever, and she made up her mind to keep an eye on the stout man.

91

The next few days were awkward, but nothing happened. *Edashla* kept on making excuses for the absence of the two older sisters, and the girl pretended to believe them. She was a hard worker and kept busy from morning until night—building, cleaning, fixing up his *nichithl*, and cutting wood like a man. The old wolverine trusted her more and more. He was sure he'd done the right thing by keeping her alive.

He took to wandering off during the day, hunting or looking over the countryside for more villages with young girls in them. So the *cushka's* daughter was left alone with her work for longer and longer periods of time.

One day while he was gone she was sitting inside the *nichithl* wondering what was going to happen, when she heard a muffled cry. At first, she couldn't figure out where it came from. Then she heard another one, but it seemed to be coming right up out of the ground from beneath the fireplace. She had almost decided that she was imagining things when she heard it again, more distinctly. She dropped onto her knees and began digging around the fireplace with her hands. Before long, she'd uncovered the hidden hole, and found her sisters.

She jumped down in and untied them while they told her who *Edashla* was, and what he planned to do to them. Since they were almost starved, she brought them something to eat.

Her first thought was that the three of them must try to escape back to the village, but before long she could see that it would never work. Her sisters barely had strength enough to talk, let alone make the long trip home.

So she made her sisters as comfortable as possible down in the pit, and brought them food and water. Then she covered them back over and made it look as though nothing had been disturbed.

When *Edashla* came back he didn't suspect anything, and life went on as usual. But several days passed before he left to go hunting again, and the girl was getting worried about her sisters.

When he finally went off one morning early, she rushed to uncover the hole to see how her sisters were. She was surprised to find they had recovered almost completely and felt well enough to risk the trip back to the village. They hurriedly grabbed what few things they would need for the trip and struck out for home. They were glad there was no snow on the ground so they wouldn't leave any tracks for *Edashla* to follow.

Late that afternoon the wolverine returned to his *nichithl*. As soon as he walked in he saw what had happened. His first thought was, "They must have run for the village. Maybe I can catch them before they make it."

So he rushed off after the three sisters as fast as he could go. The sky had clouded over, and snow began to fall in thick heavy flakes. Hardly any time at all had passed when he neared the village. It was the quickest he'd ever made the trip. But there was no sign of the girls, and he hadn't passed them on the way. Then he spotted the girls' father.

"Hello!" he called out cautiously, from a distance.

"Why, hello!" said the *cushka*. "How are you? What are you doing here, and where are my daughters?"

"Why, I left them at home," *Edashla* lied. "I thought I'd come over for a visit."

"Well, you're just in time," said the chief. "We're having a feast tonight. Why don't you go down and have a good hot steam bath, and then come on back up to the *gazhee* for dinner?"

Edashla said he'd be glad to, but as he headed for the village bathhouse, he was really confused. He kept wondering where the girls had gone if they hadn't come back to the village.

After he'd stripped off his clothes and crawled into the old log steam bath, however, *Edashla* started feeling better. There were several other men and women inside already, and they had the fire roaring. It was just right for a good hot steamer. He joined a couple of old-timers in the corner near the fire, who were taking turns switching each other with *vinik*, or branches of mountain ash. That was one of the things *Edashla* liked best about a steam bath. He'd dip a leafy branch of *vinik* in water, then slap it across his naked back until it opened up every pore, and really let the heat sink in.

One old man by the bucket kept splashing water on the rocks, and clouds of steam rolled off, to settled down over the room in blankets of suffocating heat. The steam soaked deep into *Edashla's* skin and made him forget everything but relaxing and enjoying the bath.

Several times he crawled outside and lay down to cool off. But he always went back in for more. Finally, though, he stayed inside until his face was flushed bright red and he was dizzy from the heat. Then he crawled out for the last time.

He cooled off in the dressing room and slipped on his clothes, then he headed for the *gazhee* for dinner. There was no wind and the snow was still dropping quietly through the night. *Edashla* felt completely relaxed and very hungry. He wasn't even worried any more about the girls he'd tried to kill. They were the farthest things from his mind.

As he entered the *gazhee* everyone was laughing and talking and eating, and they all seemed to be having a good time. Someone offered him a place, and he squatted down among them on some skins stretched out on the ground.

After he'd nibbled a while on the dried fish, *aguduk*, and jerky, and all the everyday foods, the *cushka* called out for the slaves to bring in the main dish. Several *noglthna* came in, carrying a huge covered platter, which they set down right in front of *Edashla*.

"Just for you!" the chief said.

A slave stepped over and lifted the top off the huge platter. At exactly the same time the *cushka's* three daughters walked

94

through the door and stood side by side staring at *Edashla*. The wolverine's eyes saw two things at once—the girls in the door, and what was on the platter. Lying there in front of him, not two feet from his nose, was a roasted human being. The villagers had killed and cooked one of their slaves for *Edashla* that afternoon after the girls had returned.

"That's what you get," cried the chief, "trying to go around eating people!"

Just then several warriors rushed through the door with spears to kill him, but before they could draw back their arms, he was already dead. For *Edashla*, the wolverine disguised as a man, was so scared he had a heart attack, and died without ever getting up off the floor.

A strange thing happened then. With his last breath *Edashla's* body shriveled up and turned back into a dirty black wolverine.

The villagers took the ugly carcass and threw it out in the woods to rot.

The Woman
and the Wolves

A LONG TIME AGO there lived a young woman whose husband never stayed home. He was always off visiting.

"I've got friends over there," he'd tell her when he didn't come in until early morning.

"What do you do?" she'd ask.

"We play games all night," he'd answer.

One day the wife's parents came to visit her.

"Where's your husband?" they asked.

"He's off visiting friends," she told them.

"No he's not," they said.

Then one of her girl friends told her, "He's over there getting married."

"Oh . . ." said the young wife. She felt very bad.

So one day soon after that, when her husband had gone, the young woman got all dressed up to leave. The last thing she did was put a feather, a magic stick, a handful of dried fish eggs, and a knife into her sewing sack.

Then she started walking. She walked and she walked, until she'd come to the very top of a mountain. She sat down there to have lunch.

While she was eating she happened to look up and see someone coming about a hundred yards off. It was her husband.

Before he could say anything she pulled the magic stick out of her sewing sack and waved it, and a canyon sprang up between them. Then she picked up her things and went on.

Her husband didn't give up, though. Several times that day when she sat down to rest, he almost caught up with her, and she had to wave the stick and make canyons or valleys between them.

Finally, late in the evening, when she'd almost lost him from sight, he called to her to come back.

"Go on home to your girl friend," she yelled. "I'm leaving you. I'm going to look for somebody else, too."

That was the last she saw of him.

A few days later the young woman came to a house where she found a young man all by himself. She was nice-looking, and he wanted her to stay, but he warned her that he had a great big wife, who was out hunting. He told her to be careful when his wife returned, because she always threw horns in the faces of young girls to kill them.

Later that evening the wife came home.

"Oh," she said. "You've got a visitor."

The big woman casually started to sit down. Then, suddenly, she turned and threw a horn into the face of the visitor.

The young woman was ready, however, and caught the horn. Then, while the huge wife was still off balance, she threw it back and killed her right there.

"Good!" said the man. "She's killed too many young women. You can stay here as long as you like."

After she'd been there a few days, however, she got tired of the man, and left.

She hadn't gone far when she met a woman who asked where

she was going. So she told the story of her husband, and why she'd left him.

The new woman shared some food with her, and while they were eating, tried to talk her into going back.

"You're a nice-looking girl," she said. "I don't know why you keep going. You're just going to destroy yourself."

"Right now, I don't care what happens to me," she answered.

When they'd finished eating, she went on her way again.

That same afternoon she came to salt water, and saw what looked like ducks out on the horizon. Looking closer, though, she saw they were *bidarkas*, or skin boats, with men in them gathering driftwood. As she lay there watching them, several turned into the bay where she was, since there was lots of driftwood in it. When they beached, some young men climbed out of the boats and started walking around picking up wood.

One of these young men walked right by her and saw the strange woman lying there watching him.

"What are you doing here?" he asked.

"Hiding."

"Who from?"

"You people are strange to me."

"Get up," he said, "and come on down to our camp. Nobody here will hurt you."

So she went down the beach with him where the others were setting up a camp.

"Where did she come from?" they asked.

The young man told them he'd found her while he was picking wood.

"Are you hungry?" they asked. Everyone was very friendly.

"Yes, I could eat," she said.

So they fed her. But while she was eating, one of the men said to her, "In a way, it's too bad we found you."

"What do you mean?" she asked.

"You're a nice-looking woman," he said. "But I'm pretty sure you're going to get killed."

"Are you fellows going to kill me?"

"No. But we've got a wife at home who always kills any girls we bring back with us."

"Oh, that's what you mean."

"Yes."

"Do you mean to tell me that just on account of her you fellows can't marry other girls?"

"That's right," he said. "You'll see."

When it came time to go, the young woman got in a *bidarka* with the man who had found her. He'd filled the boat half full with rocks.

On the way, he said to her, "They're right about that woman. She's mean and no good."

They were the last boat to come in to the beach. He'd put the rocks in on purpose to slow them down. The big ogre-woman who was their wife had come down to the beach as usual, to help pull the boats out of the water just like a man. Right away she said, "You fellows have found a woman!"

"No," they all answered.

"How come your *bidarka* is so slow?" she called to the young man.

"I'm in no hurry."

"What's the matter? Your wife too heavy? You come in to the beach so I can pull your *bidarka* up."

"I will," he said, hovering just offshore and pitching the rocks overboard.

"Here's my wife," he said, throwing a big one over the side.

That seemed to satisfy the ogre-woman, so she turned and stalked back up the hill to the house.

Right away the young man paddled ashore, jumped out, and

pulled the boat up on the beach. Then he told his new wife to wait there in the *bidarka* until after dark.

"I can't let you go up there," he said. "Later on I'll come back and take you to my mother's"

So she stayed there in the boat all that evening while he was up at the house.

Just before midnight the young man told the ogre-woman he was going to visit his mother, and returned for the young woman at the boat. Then he showed her where to walk, while he followed with some wet branches of brush, smoothing over the trail behind them.

After a while he threw the brush away and caught up with the girl.

"Why did you do that?" she asked.

"Our wife could easily smell your tracks. She's just like an animal."

When they got to his mother's, she was glad to see them, but she said to her son's new wife, "You shouldn't even be around here. If that awful woman down on the beach finds out, she'll kill you for sure."

"That's all right with me," said the young woman. She was still sad, because she really missed her first husband.

"Don't talk that way," said the old lady. "You're too young and good to be killed.

So the girl stayed with the young man's mother after that, and he came there now and then to visit them.

The young woman had never seen the ogre-wife on the beach yet, and she was getting curious about her.

"You will see her soon enough," said her husband. "Then you'll understand. But you can't go near her house, because she won't allow any other women around."

Then one morning the girl was looking out the window when the ogre-woman walked by. She had two faces.

"You've seen her?" the mother asked.

"Yes," she said.

"Now you understand why she can't be killed. She sees both ways, so nobody can sneak up behind her."

The young woman stayed there with the mother, and never left the house at all after that. A few months later she had a baby by her new husband, and raised him inside the house.

By the time the little boy was three years old, his mother had nearly gone crazy trying to hold him in the house.

So one morning when all the men had gone seal hunting, she wanted to let the boy go outside to play.

"No," said the grandmother. "He might crawl away. I don't think you'd better."

But the young woman had an idea. She tied a ten-foot piece of rawhide around the boy and fastened the other end around her waist. Then she let him out the door.

Later in the day he was seen by Two Faces, and she came over to talk to him. She couldn't get much out of the little boy, but she saw that he looked like her youngest husband. So she went back down to the house and returned with a bucket of boiling water. Setting it down right outside the door of the grandmother's house, she untied his rawhide safety line and put the little boy in the bucket.

Inside, the young mother was sewing, and not paying any attention to the line. The old grandmother said, "You ought to watch the boy more closely. At least pull on his line every now and then."

So the young mother pulled on it, and there was nothing at the other end.

Both of them ran out the door right past the bucket. Then the boy's mother looked back and saw his leg sticking out of the water. Underneath was his half-cooked body. She broke down crying. After a while, they brought what was left of the child into the house.

101

"See," said the grandmother. "That is what we warned you about."

"I'll go see her tomorrow," said the wife.

After supper, her husband came up to visit his family. His mother met him at the door.

"She killed your son."

His wife came out.

"All you fellows better say good-bye to your wife with two faces. I'm going to kill her tomorrow.

"But she might kill you instead—"

"No," she said. "I am going to kill her."

The next morning after all the men had gone hunting, she put the feather from her sewing kit in her hair, and took out the dried fish eggs and knife.

Then she told the grandmother she was going, and walked right down to the house on the beach. When she got there, she yelled, "Two Faces! You better come out and kill me. You killed my son."

"Okay. I'm coming out. You just wait. I'll kill you the same way I killed your son."

"I'm not afraid of you," yelled the young woman. "Everybody else is, but I'm not."

"I'm coming out," screamed Two Faces.

"You better come. I'm still waiting."

The ogre-woman opened the door and rushed out, but the young wife was too fast, and chopped off one of her arms with the knife. Then when Two Faces turned, she whacked off the other one. All this time she had been chewing up the dried fish eggs. Now she started spitting the juice at the raw meat. Two Faces was still screaming and thrashing around even without her arms. The young wife chopped off her head and then her legs, and kept spitting. People in those days knew that when fish egg juice was spit on an open wound, it killed more quickly than the wound itself.

102

Finally, Two Faces died. Then the young wife cut the body all up into little pieces and put them in the ogre's coat. She covered that with a blanket next and put it on the bed, leaving just the head sticking out.

When she had finished, she returned to her home at the grandmother's. The old lady had been sure she'd be killed, and was glad to see her.

"You really did kill Two Faces?"

"Yes," said the wife. "I couldn't help it, because of what she did to my son."

"Well, I won't miss her. She's killed too many people. She had it coming. I would have gone after her myself when she killed my grandson, only I'm too old. But I don't know what the men will think."

When the hunters returned, Two Faces' eldest husband was angry because she didn't come down to meet the boats. He ran up to the house and into the bedroom.

"What are you doing just lying around?" he yelled.

He started to grab her by the head, only it came off.

The rest of the brothers were there by that time, and they all just stood there looking.

The youngest one ran to his wife.

"You killed her?"

"Yes," she said.

Both of them walked back down to the beach, where she apologized to the brothers.

"I am sorry," she said. "But she killed my son."

"It's all right," said the eldest brother. "It's her own fault."

After that the young woman stayed in the house on the beach, and cooked for the brothers and looked after them just like Two Faces had. But before long she started getting lonely.

One night while the men were off hunting she felt especially bad, so she went up to visit her husband's mother.

"You're from a different tribe," the old lady said.

"Yes, I know."

"It might be best if you don't stay here. Those brothers may try to kill you."

"Are they talking about it?"

"I haven't heard them, but I know their minds. They're my sons, but they've got their own minds."

"I'd better go," the young woman decided.

So the old grandma explained to her how to find her way out of the country.

"Go until you come to a creek. Walk right into it, and follow it all the way up the mountain."

The next nice day, the young wife started off. But she didn't believe the old woman's warning about walking in the creek. She just climbed way up to the top of a mountain in the direction of home. Then, since it was so nice, she sat down and took out her sewing. After a while she got tired and fell asleep.

When she woke up someone was shaking her. It was the young man who had found her on the beach.

"What are you doing up here?" he asked. "You were sleeping."

She couldn't answer him.

"You'd better go back down with me. It's getting cold."

She started to get up.

"Were you trying to go home?"

"No," she said. "It was such a nice day I just wanted to sit up here to do my sewing."

So they went back down the mountain and she cooked supper as usual.

After the meal was finished, the young woman went to visit Grandma.

"Did you try to go home?" the old lady asked.

"Yes."

"How did you go?"

"Up the mountain."

"I told you to follow the creeks," the old woman said, "because the boys can smell your tracks."

The young woman believed her now. But it was a long while before the brothers went out hunting again. This time she packed up and left in a hurry, for she was beginning to be afraid. She followed the beach until she came to a creek, then walked in it all the way up the mountain. When she reached the top, she sat down to watch the house on the beach.

She could see the *bidarkas* when the men came back from hunting. As soon as they hit the beach, everybody got out and walked up to the house. In a minute they all hurried back outside and started looking around. Then they began fighting each other. They moved back into the house as the fight got worse. Finally, just before dark, the young woman saw the house quake and cave in.

The next morning she waited until daylight, but no smoke rose from the house on the beach. So she walked back down the mountain.

The house was in shambles, and the roof had fallen in. There was no fire, and no noise. When she put her head inside she found the ten dead bodies of the brothers, and that of the grandmother. Now the young woman knew why they could smell her tracks so easily. The bodies were those of wolves. They had all turned back into their real selves when they killed each other.

The young woman cried for some time. She really felt bad. She thought it would have been better if they'd killed her rather than themselves.

When she'd finished crying, she went over to the cache and picked out all the nice meat. She got plenty to live on. Then, once more, she started walking back to where she'd come from, along the shoreline.

After two days the young woman came to a *nichithl* a few steps away from the beach. When she went inside, she found an older man.

105

"Come in," he said. "It looks like you've come a long ways."

Later on he told her, "You were married once, and not doing too bad. Then you took off, and now you're leading a miserable life."

She waited until he was finished.

"You're right," she said.

The young woman stayed there after that, and the old-timer was good to her, but she was always a little bit afraid of him. She couldn't run away, though, because he never went out hunting in the boat. He did hunt once in a while, but he was never gone long, and never went out on the water.

One day she said to her new husband, "I don't feel well. I'd like to stay by myself. I'll come to visit you, but I'd like a house of my own."

"O.K.," he said. "I'll build you a little house. Where do you want it?"

"Down on the beach," she said. "Right on top of the bank."

"How come right by the beach?"

"I like to listen to the wind, and the water splashing up on the shore."

"Oh," he said, and built her little house just as she wanted it, right on the bank.

When the young woman had moved into her new home, she felt a lot better, and visited the old man enough so he wouldn't get angry.

She stayed there for more than a year. She would have liked to go back home to her first husband, but she was lost and didn't know which way that was.

Late one evening, just before midnight, she was sewing by the light of her grease lamp. It was flat calm outside and she heard a *bidarka* beaching just below her little house. Then the skin door of her *nichithl* opened, and in walked her first husband! He had finally caught up with her.

106

"I've been looking for you all this time," he said. "I want you to come back with me."

He had left the other woman for good, and promised he would be faithful to his wife now.

"How did you find me?" she asked.

"While I was coming, I met different people and asked after you. Then I heard about a woman that might be you. I was just going to stop here and ask again, but now I've found you."

She told him not to speak too loudly because of the other man.

So they gathered up her things quietly and rowed out to sea in the *bidarka*.

The trip home took several days. By that time everyone in the village had heard what had happened to her. And they were all happy to have her home again.

The Mink Story

ONE TIME there was an old woman who lived alone with her grandson on an island. The boy's parents had died, and he grew up supporting his grandma. They never left the island or saw anyone else.

One day when he was out hunting along the beach, the boy found some wood chips that had drifted in from across the water somewhere.

"I wonder," he thought, "if there are other people in the world besides us."

So he ran home to ask his grandma. "Are we the only ones on earth, or are there other people like us?"

"There are others," she said. "Have you seen someone?"

He showed her the chips. "That's how I found out," he said.

"There are people around," she told him. "But they are a long way off, and it is hard to get there. If you want to go see them, you must first get me lots of wood."

So the boy ran off and started cutting wood for his grandma,

108

taking time out only to hunt enough to keep them alive, for almost two years.

Meantime, the old woman took out her sewing kit and started making a *bidarka*, or skin boat, for him. She took little hides from game they had trapped and shook them until they got bigger, then she sewed them together. After the boy had gathered enough firewood to last her for a long time, he helped her finish the boat.

Then he made extra spears, bows, and arrows, which his grandmother had shown him how to use. He could even kill sea otters with them.

Finally, before he left to go look for the other people, the boy stored up plenty of food for his grandma to eat.

The last thing before he went, she took a piece of string out of her sewing kit to give to him. It was very long and all piled up in a bunch; and right on the end of it was a whole mink skin with the skull still inside.

"Do you know what this is for?" she asked him.

"No."

"In the wintertime, if you really get stuck, you'll need this. It can catch trout or salmon or little animals for you. Put it right in your shirt, and if anything happens, don't be afraid to use it. But don't ever let anyone find out you have it."

So he did as he was told. Then he got in the boat and started off. The water was long and the time passed slowly. But finally he could see things getting big on the other side.

That evening the tide carried him right in to the beach, and when he hit shore, two boys came down and grabbed his *bidarka* and pulled him in.

He got out and shook hands with the boys, and they were glad to see him. They all liked each other.

"Let's go up to the house," the boys said, leading the way.

It turned out that they were the chief's sons, and he was a very rich man.

"Where did you get this strange boy?" the *cushka* asked them.

"He's our friend now," they said. "He just came in."

"So you're a stranger here?"

"Yes."

"You're the one who supports your grandmother?"

"Yes," he said, surprised.

The chief told the boy they had heard about him, and said he could stay there with his two sons.

At suppertime the boy found out the *cushka* had a pretty daughter. After she had cooked the meal, she said:

"I sure wish I had caribou meat for supper tomorrow night."

The brothers told him not to pay any attention to her. "She always says that."

Later that night, however, he happened to be standing alone with the girl, and she reminded him that she was the chief's daughter, and said if he didn't bring her what she wanted, she'd tell the village people to kill him. She was used to having her own way.

So early the next morning the boy went out in the hills and shot two caribou. When he'd eaten the liver and washed it down with tea, he packed the rest back to the house.

The chief's daughter met him at the door. She seemed quite happy as she grabbed the pack and rushed in to cook the meat.

"You must have gone a long way to get that," she said.

"I did," he replied.

That evening, as she dished out the caribou meat for supper, she said, "I sure wish I had some fresh seal for tomorrow night."

She liked a different kind of meat every day.

It was falltime, however, and seals were hard to find. The next day the stranger looked and looked before he found one. Then he killed it and ate the liver, and packed the meat home in the skin.

Again, the girl was happy about it, but that night while they

110

were eating she mentioned she would like *muktuk* for dinner the next day.

The two brothers were angry, but the stranger went out in his *bidarka* the next morning to get what she wanted. It was hard this time, but finally he got two whales and brought plenty of *muktuk* back. His two friends met him at the beach as usual, and helped to pull his boat in.

It was getting colder every night now since it was so late in the fall, and everyone was surprised at supper when the daughter said (while she was dishing out the *muktuk*), "I sure wish I had a groundhog."

The stranger almost dropped his plate. The mountains were far away, and it was pretty late in the season to be hunting groundhogs.

The boy was so worried he didn't even sleep that night, and the next morning he took off quite early. He went clear back to the mountains, and by the time he got there he was already sorry he'd come. He couldn't think where he would find a groundhog.

Finally he saw one sitting on a rock, so he slung his arrow and sneaked up on it. When he shot, the groundhog jumped up wounded, and ran back into his hole.

The boy didn't know what to do. Then he remembered the mink skin. He pulled it out and stuffed it down into the hole. The skin turned into a live mink and ran off after the groundhog, while the boy paid out the line behind it. After a while, the string quit running out and started twitching. When it stopped, he pulled it out—the mink first, then the groundhog. The mink died into a skin again and he tucked it into his shirt. The groundhog had died too, way back down the hole, and he stuffed it into his pack.

Then he sat down for a while, thinking.

"No wonder Grandma gave me this."

When he went back, the boys met him at the beach and were

glad to see he was still alive. The girl grabbed the pack and had the hog half skinned by the time he got inside. She was happy again.

By now it was winter and everything had frozen solid. There was ice all over.

At supper the chief's good-looking daughter said:

"I sure wish I had fresh king salmon for tomorrow night."

The stranger almost fainted.

"I guess she'll just have to kill me," he thought.

The next morning, though, he went out very early with a little sleigh and a net. He put the net down through a pressure crack, but the weather was so cold that when he pulled it up, the net was frozen stiff. He didn't know what to do. Then he thought of the mink skin.

So he set it down into the water, and it came to life and dived under. The boy paid out the string behind as it swam away beneath the ice. Then it stopped, and the string began to go forth and back sideways. When it stopped, the boy started pulling it in. It was quite heavy.

When the mink came in sight, he saw that it had caught a big king salmon, so he speared the fish and pulled it up on the ice.

The young hunter was glad that he'd gotten it, but he wondered, "What next?"

He put the fish on the sledge with the net and went home.

The boys were glad to see him again, but the chief's daughter ran out and grabbed the pack before he could even get it off his back.

"You got the king salmon, huh? Well, hurry up and get in the house."

She'd never done that before. Even the *cushka* was surprised.

So the stranger went inside and sat down, but when he started to take his boots off, she said, "No!" and ran to him and *she* took them off.

After she had dished out supper for everyone, she sat down

beside him and started eating from the same plate he was eating from.

The boy was still worried though, and he couldn't eat at all.

"Don't worry," she told him. "You won't ever have to go hunting again."

Then she said that she was going to marry him, and everyone was happy.

The very next morning they got married, and she gave him a parka and mukluks, and treated him like a king. He didn't even have to dress himself. She gave him everything he wanted.

After that the boy was happy living there in the village.

But by the time two years had passed, he was a little homesick.

"Do you want to go home?" his wife asked him.

"Yes," he said. "I'd like to go see my grandma again."

"O.K.," she said. "Let's go."

So that spring they went back to the island. When they saw smoke coming up from the little house, they knew his grandma was still alive.

She was really surprised to see them. She'd been worried about her grandson.

The young couple lived there on the island for almost a year, until the old lady died. Then they returned to the girl's village where her husband became a very rich man, and later on, chief.

The Trout Story

THERE WAS ONCE a woman whose husband mistreated her so much that she left home. She walked and walked until she came to a strange village far away from her home country. When she entered the *gazhee*, she didn't see anyone around, but there were lots of beds, so she picked one out and went to sleep on it.

While she slept, a woman came out of the other room and made her a lunch. When it was finished, the woman woke her and told her to sit up and eat.

"You sure picked the wrong bed!" she said.

"Why is that?" the stranger asked.

"It's the custom here that whosever bed you sleep on, you marry," the village woman answered. "That's my son's bed, but he never stays home. He just goes and goes all the time."

That night everyone in the village came back to the *gazhee*. All his brothers were there, but the son on whose bed the stranger had slept didn't come home. The brothers all said, "You sure picked out the wrong bed. Why did you pick that one?"

114

"I just like the way it looks," she said.

"You might as well marry the bed," they told her. "He doesn't even hunt. You'll see!"

All the brothers had meat hanging outside, but he'd never even killed a spruce chicken.

When he finally came home, they told him that the stranger was his new wife. He didn't seem very excited.

"What do you do all day?" she asked him.

"I sleep," he said.

"Can't you just sleep at home in your bed, since you don't hunt anyway?"

"No," he said. "That's just me."

"Well, where do you sleep?" she asked.

"In trees."

The young woman was really puzzled.

He said she could be his wife, but he warned her never to look at him too closely.

"Don't even sit close to me," he warned.

"O.K.," she said.

As time went by, he continued to stay away from the village as much as possible. He wouldn't come back any more than he had to.

Finally one of his brothers told the woman, "I found out where he spends all his time . . . but you'll never get him. He stays at the top of a big tree with a fish hawk-woman."

His wife was very angry.

"I'll fix him," she thought.

The next day she set to work and made a long thick snare. Then she went looking for him. After a while she found the tree the others had told her about. It was so big her husband couldn't even climb up and down it. The fish hawk-woman would just turn herself into a bird whenever he came and fly him to the top. Then when he wanted to leave, she would fly him back down to the ground.

The young woman cut a long stick and tied the snare onto it. She could just barely see her husband's feet hanging down out of the branches at the top. But when she tried to reach him with the snare, she found that the stick was too short, so she had to cut another one. This one reached.

She snared him by the feet and pulled him down out of the tree. Then she told him to "get home." She was a pretty stout woman.

When they got back to the village, the others told her, "That's fine, but what are you going to do about the fish hawk-woman? There's no way you can reach her."

"Oh," she said. "I'll take care of her."

The next morning when the fish hawk-woman wasn't around, the young wife went out and started cutting down the tree with an ax. She chopped until it was just about ready to fall.

That night, when she was sure the fish hawk-woman was asleep up in the tree, the young wife went back and pushed it over. The tree smashed into the ground before the fish hawk-woman could wake up and she was killed. When the young wife walked over to look at the body she saw that the woman had changed back into a fish hawk. So she plucked all the feathers off it and put them into her purse before going back to the village.

Early the next morning when her husband started to leave as usual, she said to him, "What's your hurry? You don't have to rush off. Your nest is knocked down."

"What do you mean?" he asked.

"I killed the fish hawk-woman."

But her husband just laughed at her; and when his brothers and the other villagers found out, they laughed too.

"You couldn't kill the fish hawk-woman," they said. "Nobody can hurt *her*!"

Then she pulled out the feathers and held them up.

"Those are hers," she said.

So they all ran out and looked, and found that it was true.

After that, the husband stayed at home for quite a while. By and by, however, he started going out fishing every day. It got just like before. Then his brothers told her, "He's gone again, and you can't get him back this time. Do you know what he's doing?"

"No," she said.

"He's staying with a fish-woman. He can't even get away himself now. He tried. You can see him down in the water, but you can't get him back."

"Oh, I can easily get him back," she said.

She reached into her purse and pulled out the feathers of the fish hawk-woman. Then she went back to where she used to live and got some fish eggs and Indian beads. After that she made a snare.

By this time it was winter and she carried her things out on the river ice. Looking through a hole in the ice, she saw a house way down at the bottom of the water. Her husband was in there with that fish-woman.

First she threw some beads down in the hole to attract their attention. Then she threw in the fish eggs. As they sank down into the house, her husband and the fish-woman jumped up and started catching and eating them. So she reached down into the water and snared both of them, and pulled them out onto the ice. She killed the fish-woman, who turned into a trout, but her husband just slept.

She woke him up and told him, "This is the last time I'm coming after you. The next time I won't feel sorry for you; I'll just kill you."

She was large, and she pushed him.

"Now you get home," she said.

On the way back to the village she tried to make him feel ashamed.

"Don't you ever think about your mother? Your brothers all get meat and take care of her, but what do you do? Nothing! Hurry up and get home!"

He said he was sorry and really thanked her for saving his life. In fact, when they got back to the village and everyone was surprised to see him, he told his mother and brothers, "She rescued me and saved my life. I'll stay home for sure now."

But the wife still didn't trust him and said to his mother, "He'd better. Because the next time I won't save him. I'll kill him."

She turned to him and said, "I'm going to make you into a man, so you can go out and make a living like your brothers."

But she didn't have to say all those things. He really was thankful she'd saved him, and promised that he would straighten out.

And he did.

The Beaver
and the Porcupine Woman

ONCE THERE WAS a porcupine-woman who wanted to go snare squirrels on a mountain that lay on the other side of the river from her home. Since she couldn't swim she asked a beaver to take her across the water.

"Sure," said the beaver. "Climb on."

So she got on his back and he started swimming across. Just before they reached the other bank, however, she said, "Oh, I forgot my snares. Could you take me back across for a minute?"

"I guess so," the beaver said. But the porcupine-woman was certainly heavy.

He took her back though, and waited for her while she got her snares. Then she settled herself on his back again and he struck out for the other side. But just before they got there she said, "Wait a minute! I forgot my needle case. We have to go back."

So the beaver turned around and recrossed the river. By this time he was really getting tired. The porcupine-woman was pretty stout.

"All right, let's go," she said when she returned with her needle case.

When she got on his back this time the beaver's head went almost completely under water because he was so tired and she was so fat. But he took off, and they nearly reached the opposite bank before she remembered she'd forgotten her cane.

"Oh, say," she said, "I forgot . . ."—but the beaver rolled right over and spilled her into the water.

The porcupine-woman splashed and splashed, until she finally managed to get ashore, where she crawled up out of the water onto a bear trail. The beaver emerged right behind her, and she turned without saying a word and pounced. She quilled him up pretty bad before she left. He probably died.

The Flounder Story

A RICH MAN over on the saltwater side once had a daughter so pretty men were always trying to marry her. Even her grandma was jealous of how much attention she got.

One morning the rich man and his wife left the house to go mountain squirrel trapping. As soon as they had gone the old grandma walked out onto the hillside and cut up lots of berries. When she had enough, she took them over to a corner of land sticking out into the water and scattered the berries all around in the turf. Then she took her knife and cut a deep groove across the inside of the little point.

When she went back to the house, the old woman told the rich man's daughter there were lots of berries out on that point, and the girl ran out to pick some. She was so happy to find that many berries in one place that she wasn't paying any attention to what was going on around her and didn't notice when the tide came in and the piece of turf broke off and started floating out to sea. By the time she looked up, the current had carried her for miles into strange country where no one from her family had ever been.

That night, while the rich man's daughter was sleeping, a strong wind came up and pushed the little block of ground into the far shore. When it struck land she woke up and saw how rough the sea was getting, and that she was near a cave on the face of a rock cliff that dropped straight into the water. She was afraid, so she took some berries along for food and jumped off into the cave. Soon the turf had drifted away and pounded to pieces on the rocks at the foot of the cliff.

It didn't take long for the girl to realize that she was in a tough spot. There was no way out of the cave except into the water or up the face of the cliff. The tide was coming in and it wouldn't be long before the whole bluff would be under water. She was trapped. The rich man's daughter lay down at the mouth of the cave beside the rising water and started crying.

Not long after that a man was passing by in a *bidarka* when he saw the fancy red fringe from her parka floating in the water beside the cave, so he paddled over and found the rich man's daughter in there still crying. He told her to come home with him. The girl couldn't see his face because it was dark, but she really liked the sound of his voice, and he smelled of *shucktuzha*, which was a rare perfume from a plant way up in the mountains only rich men could afford to get, so she thought it would be all right. He said they would have to hurry, however, because he wanted to be home by midnight, although he didn't say why.

The reason for his rush was that he was really only a slave of two rich men, and he had to be in by that time. He and his grandma lived in a house out under the slop pile, and every day he had to go out and hunt for young girls for his masters. They gave him a boat, food, *shucktuzha*, and everything else he needed to attract women, but he was still just a slave.

Only this time he decided he would keep the rich man's daughter for himself, and not tell her about the two rich, handsome men he worked for. And by the time they got back to where he lived, she found out he was mean.

"Get out of the boat," he told her. "Go on up to the house."

After he had pulled the boat up on the beach, he brought a pair of seal lungs up to the house, and he and his grandma ate them raw. They gave some to the girl too, but she didn't care much for it.

He told her the only time she could go outside was when he was at home at midnight. He said there were other people around who were really mean, even if they did sound nice from a distance sometimes.

The next morning when he got up to go out hunting for a girl for his masters, the rich man's daughter was awake and saw him in the light. He was very ugly and had only one eye right in the middle of his face, and the eye was filled with pus. There was a basket below his eye catching the pus as it drained out. By now his *shucktuzha* had worn off, and he smelled terrible. Then she knew that he was a flounder-man.

For almost a week, though, she stayed in the house under the slop pile during the day and went out only at night. But she finally got to hating the filth and smell and raw seal lungs so much she sneaked out one afternoon while the flounder-man was hunting and the grandma was sleeping. In the bright sunlight she was surprised to see a nice house and cache. She walked over to them, and a woman found her there and asked her where she had come from, so the rich man's daughter told her all about the flounder-man.

"Come inside," said the woman. "Now you'll be the wife of two nice good-looking men."

So the girl followed her into the house and the woman brought her hot water so she could wash and clean up. Pretty soon the rich men came home. When she had told them her story, they wanted to go down and kill the flounder-man, but she wouldn't let them. Instead, when he came home with a load of meat, they didn't go down to help him hang it up and clean out his boat, but the rich man's daughter went, dressed in nice clothes and looking pretty, and she teased the flounder-man and made fun of him and told him how ugly he was. He couldn't even talk back to her because he knew his masters would get after him.

The next day the two men took the girl back to where she'd come from. Her parents had been crying all the time she was gone. When she told her father what the grandma had done, he took the old woman out back of the house to a little flat spot and clubbed her to death.

The two rich men stayed there with the girl about two months. Then they gave her folks lots of food and supplies and went home —and the rich man's daughter went with them as their wife.

Glossary of Non-English Words
Used in the Text*

aguduk: (ah goo′ duk) actually an Eskimo word, it is habitually used by the Indians in place of their own *nuvagee* (nuh vah′ gee) to mean a cold dish usually consisting of blueberries, blackberries, or low-bush cranberries mixed with sugar and some form of grease— traditionally moose fat, seal oil, or bear grease, but in modern times usually shortening or lard; loosely, "Eskimo ice cream"

alutika: (ah loo′ tuh kuh) spruce needle

barabara: (bah rob′ ur ee) Russian word for the Indian *nichithl*—a circular poled skin house similar to the *gazhee*, but smaller

bidarka: (bi dar′ kee) Indian skin boat on the order of an Eskimo kayak, with one or a pair of holes in which to sit; the openings were tied around a warrior's waist to make the craft waterproof; those who were expert at handling a *bidarka* could flip one upside down and right it again with no difficulty, which proved useful for passing enemies on a riverbank, or in rough seas

chada: (chah′ dah) old man or grandfather

chulyen: (chool′ yen) invariably translated from the Kenai as "crow,"

* Athapascan if not otherwise indicated.

the bird to which it refers is a raven; that is, the bird found in the Cook Inlet-Lake Iliamna area of Alaska is of the species *Corvus corax*, not *Corvus brachyrynchos*, though both are of the crow family, Corvidae; the raven is the larger of the two; the *Chulyen* who is a distinct character in Kenai mythology is credited with having made the world

cushka: (kush kah') rich man or chief; he had more clothes (skins) than anyone else in the village, and slaves captured from other tribes—or poor members of his own village—to do his work; the *cushka* sometimes lived apart from the rest of the village in a private *nichithl* in preference to the communal *gazhee*

cushkaveah: (kush kah' vee yah) rich man's son

dukhoe: (dukh' oe) war club made from the leg of a moose

edah: (ee' dah) "pal"; diminutive of *edashla*; the Indians used to refer to the wolverine as "pal"

edashla: (ee dah' shlah) wolverine

gazhee: (gah' zhee) circular poled skin house in which the whole village community used to live together; there was a hole in the middle of the roof under which the fire was built, so that the dwelling was heated uniformly; each family laid its several sleeping sacks out close together in the night, then rolled them up the next morning and stacked them along the wall; there were two doors, usually, one at either end; the larger villages were composed of several *gazhees*

joncha: (jon' chah) the secret animal identity into which a person may transform himself; may be anything from a mouse to a bear, or a fish to an eagle; according to Indian legend, everyone is born with a *joncha*, and once a person finds out what his *joncha* is, he may change into that animal at any time—but he is subject to its handicaps as well as its advantages

kashna: (kah' jhnah) lynx; means "black spot" in Kenai

kentah: (k' en tah') the juice rendered when salmon eggs are crushed; said by the old Kenai to cause immediate death when spit on or applied to an open wound

kichivkooya: (ki" chiv koo' yah) old lady or grandma of the village who often lived apart from the others in her own *nichithl*, sometimes with a young boy; she was revered as being very wise

kon: ([s]kon) mice colony

kongaloshee: (kon' gah lo shee) long vine-type root found in thick brushy woods; this "Indian rope," as it is called, is strong and supple and may be braided so that it will support a very great weight; found to lengths of fifty feet

Kuskadanee Sabaka: (kus" kah dah' nee se bahck' ah) "Kuskokwim Dogs"—the Indian name for the Eskimos who inhabited First Bethel, who were reputed to have killed one another over food

muktuk: (muk' tuk) an Eskimo word used by the Kenai to mean whale blubber

nichithl: (ni chithl') miniature model of the communal *gazhee*; this small circular poled hut was the one in which the *cushka* or *kichivkooya* lived separated from the rest of the village

nikaseenithulooyee: (neh kah tsi" nee thl oo' yee) "animal that's half on the beach and half in the water"; translated variously as an alligator, sea turtle, or land otter by Kenai today, as no one alive seems to know to what animal it referred originally

noglthna: (no' glthl nah") slave; usually captured from other tribes, but the term is also used in reference to the poorer members of a village who worked for their room and board for the *cushka*, or "rich man"

shucktuzha: (shuckh too' zha) rare perfume from a plant found only high in the mountains; rich men, who alone could afford the time and expense of obtaining it, sent slaves to find and bring it back

skaga: (skah' gah) chickadee

suk-tu: (sook' too) translated literally as "legend-story" by the Kenais; distinct from both historical events and truly believed cultural mythology, today these stories are not believed to have really happened by anyone except by small children, although the stories are told as if they had happened

vajich: (vah' jickh) caribou

vinik: (vin' ick) mountain ash; the old-timers used branches of this to switch themselves in steambaths because it opened the pores and let heat penetrate

vittuh: (vit' tuh) shirt or jacket sleeve

vok: (vahch) sea gull

vudee: (vud' ee) Aleut skin boat, similar to *bidarka*

The Civilization
of the
American Indian
Series

of which *Tanaina Tales from Alaska* is the ninety-sixth volume, was inaugurated in 1932 by the University of Oklahoma Press, and has as its purpose the reconstruction of American Indian civilization by presenting aboriginal, historical, and contemporary Indian life. The following list is complete as of the date of publication of this volume.

1. *Forgotten Frontiers:* A Study of the Spanish Indian Policy of Don Juan Bautista de Anza, Governor of New Mexico, 1777–1787. Translated and edited by Alfred Barnaby Thomas.
2. Grant Foreman. *Indian Removal:* The Emigration of the Five Civilized Tribes of Indians.
3. John Joseph Mathews. *Wah'Kon-Tah:* The Osage and the White Man's Road.
4. Grant Foreman. *Advancing the Frontier, 1830–1860.*
5. John H. Seger. *Early Days Among the Cheyenne and Arapahoe Indians.* Edited by Stanley Vestal.
6. Angie Debo. *The Rise and Fall of the Choctaw Republic.*

7. Stanley Vestal. *New Sources of Indian History, 1850–1891:* A Miscellany. Out of print.
8. Grant Foreman. *The Five Civilized Tribes.*
9. *After Coronado:* Spanish Exploration Northeast of New Mexico, 1696–1727. Translated and edited by Alfred Barnaby Thomas.
10. Frank G. Speck, *Naskapi:* The Savage Hunters of the Labrador Peninsula. Out of print.
11. Elaine Goodale Eastman. *Pratt:* The Red Man's Moses. Out of print.
12. Althea Bass. *Cherokee Messenger:* A Life of Samuel Austin Worcester.
13. Thomas Wildcat Alford. *Civilization.* As told to Florence Drake. Out of print.
14. Grant Foreman. *Indians and Pioneers:* The Story of the American Southwest Before 1830.
15. George E. Hyde. *Red Cloud's Folk:* A History of the Oglala Sioux Indians.
16. Grant Foreman. *Sequoyah.*
17. Morris L. Wardell. *A Political History of the Cherokee Nation, 1838–1907.* Out of print.
18. John Walton Caughey. *McGillivray of the Creeks.*
19. Edward Everett Dale and Gaston Litton. *Cherokee Cavaliers:* Forty Years of Cherokee History as Told in the Correspondence of the Ridge-Watie-Boudinot Family. Out of print.
20. Ralph Henry Gabriel. *Elias Boudinot, Cherokee, and His America.* Out of print.
21. Karl N. Llewellyn and E. Adamson Hoebel. *The Cheyenne Way:* Conflict and Case Law in Primitive Jurisprudence.
22. Angie Debo. *The Road to Disappearance.*
23. Oliver La Farge and others. *The Changing Indian.* Out of print.
24. Carolyn Thomas Foreman. *Indians Abroad.* Out of print.
25. John Adair. *The Navajo and Pueblo Silversmiths.*
26. Alice Marriott. *The Ten Grandmothers.*
27. Alice Marriott. *María:* The Potter of San Ildefonso.
28. Edward Everett Dale. *The Indians of the Southwest:* A Century of Development Under the United States. Out of print.

130

51. C. L. Sonnichsen. *The Mescalero Apaches.*
52. Keith A. Murray. *The Modocs and Their War.*
53. *The Incas of Pedro de Cieza de León.* Edited by Victor Wolfgang von Hagen and translated by Harriet de Onis.
54. George E. Hyde. *Indians of the High Plains:* From the Prehistoric Period to the Coming of Europeans.
55. *George Catlin:* Episodes from "Life Among the Indians" and "Last Rambles." Edited by Marvin C. Ross.
56. J. Eric S. Thompson. *Maya Hieroglyphic Writing:* An Introduction.
57. George E. Hyde. *Spotted Tail's Folk:* A History of the Brulé Sioux.
58. James Larpenteur Long. *The Assiniboines:* From the Accounts of the Old Ones Told to First Boy (James Larpenteur Long). Edited and with an introduction by Michael Stephen Kennedy.
59. Edwin Thompson Denig. *Five Indian Tribes of the Upper Missouri:* Sioux, Arickaras, Assiniboines, Crees, Crows. Edited and with an introduction by John C. Ewers.
60. John Joseph Mathews. *The Osages:* Children of the Middle Waters.
61. Mary Elizabeth Young. *Redskins, Ruffleshirts, and Rednecks:* Indian Allotments in Alabama and Mississippi, 1830–1860.
62. J. Eric S. Thompson. *A Catalog of Maya Hieroglyphs.*
63. Mildred P. Mayhall. *The Kiowas.*
64. George E. Hyde. *Indians of the Woodlands:* From Prehistoric Times to 1725.
65. Grace Steele Woodward. *The Cherokees.*
66. Donald J. Berthrong. *The Southern Cheyennes.*
67. Miguel León-Portilla. *Aztec Thought and Culture:* A Study of the Ancient Nahuatl Mind. Translated by Jack Emory Davis.
68. T. D. Allen. *Navahos Have Five Fingers.*
69. Burr Cartwright Brundage. *Empire of the Inca.*
70. A. M. Gibson. *The Kickapoos:* Lords of the Middle Border.
71. Hamilton A. Tyler. *Pueblo Gods and Myths.*
72. Royal B. Hassrick. *The Sioux:* Life and Customs of a Warrior Society.

132

94. Gottfried Hotz. *Eighteenth-Century Skin Paintings*. Translated by Johannes Malthaner.
95. Virgil J. Vogel. *American Indian Medicine*.
96. Bill Vaudrin. *Tanaina Tales from Alaska*. With an introduction by Joan Broom Townsend.

TANAINA TALES FROM ALASKA was set on the Linotype in eleven-point Old Style, a typeface selected for its compactness, even color, and uncommon legibility.

Display type is Helvetica, a handsome twentieth-century face chosen for its graceful lines and classic simplicity.

Silhouettes at chapter openings were especially traced for this book from cave paintings found on Cook Inlet and thought to be originally made by Kenai Indians.

The paper on which this book is printed bears the watermark of the University of Oklahoma Press and has an effective life of at least three hundred years.

UNIVERSITY OF OKLAHOMA PRESS

NORMAN